Diego's Story

MIRROR BOOKS

Names and locations have been changed throughout in order to protect the identities of individuals.

1

Published in Great Britain and Ireland in 2026 by
Mirror Books, a Reach PLC business,
5 St Paul's Square, Liverpool, L3 9SJ.

www.mirrorbooks.co.uk
@TheMirrorBooks

Print ISBN 9781917439732
eBook ISBN 9781917439749

Design and production by Mirror Books.

Printed and bound in Great Britain by
CPI Group (UK) Ltd, Croydon, CR0 4YY

Cover image: Adobe Stock
(Posed by model)

This book was printed using
FSC approved materials.

FSC www.fsc.org MIX Paper | Supporting responsible forestry FSC® C013604

THROWN AWAY CHILDREN

Diego's Story

07811607187

Louise Allen

with Theresa McEvoy

MIRROR BOOKS

The cases I reveal in my books are all based on true experiences, but I have changed names and some details to protect their identities as they go on to build new lives and families of their own.

Foreword

This is the 13th book in the *Thrown Away Children* series, a collection which tells the stories of some of the 30 or so children who have spent time being fostered in the Allen household.

Diego grew up in Liverpool at a time when it was the third most deprived local authority in England, with 63% of residents living in areas ranked among the most deprived in the country, and three in 10 children deemed to be living in poverty.

Growing up in poverty has long-term impacts on children's health, social and educational outcomes. Poverty is strongly associated with poorer physical and mental health, including increased risks of chronic illness, anxiety and depression. Educationally, children living in poverty start school with lower levels of vocabulary, motor skills, literacy and numeracy and rarely catch up with their classmates, leaving school with fewer academic qualifications than their peers. Socially, they are less likely to experience the kinds of enriching activities that contribute to personal development and social mobility. They are automatically and involuntarily enrolled into a lifetime cycle of poverty, reduced employment prospects and the increased likelihood of unemployment.

But, for some reason, we as a society seem to do little to tackle the problem head on. And all the while, the true, long-term cost to us all of having children growing up in poverty continues to rack up. A major new piece of research is planned to begin in 2026. Thousands of babies will be enrolled in the Generation New Era study to track them through infancy and beyond. The project will look at things like parental employment, childcare rates, language acquisition, school-readiness and even body-fat ratios. One of the outcomes will be to shed light on the myriad of ways that poverty affects children.

Sadly, the cost of living crisis in recent years has had a more direct impact on children. Beyond the broad challenges of living in poverty, it has also made them more vulnerable to exploitation through county lines.

County lines refers to gangs who move, hold, and sell drugs across the UK. It's known as county lines because, originally, children were forced to travel across counties and use dedicated mobile phone 'lines' to deliver drugs as part of organised crime rings. These days, with much larger networks, that might not necessarily be the case as distribution of drugs becomes more localised.

It's immaterial; it's all a form of criminal exploitation. All illegal drugs distributed in the UK have more than likely passed through a county line. In order for this to happen, vast numbers of people are required. The scale of county lines operations is *vast*. And the people that are used to run it on the ground are those who need money and won't ask questions. Unfortunately, the demographic that best meets this criteria is made up of children and vulnerable adults.

According to figures from The Children's Society, an estimated 46,000 children in England are believed to be involved in gangs. That is an enormous number. Diego was one of those children. It was his misfortune to become involved; it was not his fault.

Diego is, of course, not his real name, nor the other name he shares with us. As with all the children I write about, their identity is disguised in order to protect them. Details are changed to ensure anonymity, while attempting to preserve the facts of the story. Never has that been more important than in this story.

Diogo Jota is mentioned several times during *Diego's Story*. His full name was Diogo José Teixeira da Silva and he was a Portuguese professional footballer who sadly died in a car crash in 2025, aged 28. He played for Liverpool Football Club and was an important and influential player, pivotal to the success of both his club and country in recent years.

I

PART ONE

Liverpool

The boy opens his eyes and stretches out his arms. It's definitely morning, because light is coming through the thin curtains, but he still feels tired. When he thinks about how tired he feels, he senses another lion-yawn building. It takes over his whole body. Even his hands spasm as he yawns. With his arms still outstretched, he catches sight of his own underarm hair. The dark curls are another reminder, as if he needed them, that he is almost a man; soon to be 13.

He *is* the man of this family because he is the oldest now that his father is not around.

He looks across to the other side of his room where his brother, Andre, is still sleeping. The younger boys, Dinis and Tomas, share a bunk bed in the box room. Andre is 11 and will start at the same school as his big brother in September, after the summer holidays. He wishes their dad was here, to be able to see Andre and be proud of him starting at big school. He wishes his dad was here full stop.

Most of all, he would like to play football with his dad once more. Duarte was a good footballer. Family folklore says that he might have made the big league if an injury hadn't stopped his career just at the wrong moment. He was really good when he was young, so good that, for a short while, he played professionally for his local team. The name Duarte Pereira might have been as famous as Cristiano Ronaldo, but when he hurt his knee, that was that.

The boy would like to be as good as his father one day.

The hours spent playing football in the park with his dad are among his happiest memories.

The other happy memories are of spectating. Watching football on the TV with his dad. Best of all, the three times they were lucky enough to go to Anfield to see a match live.

Liverpool, the greatest team in Europe.

It's one of the reasons that his father chose Liverpool as the city for them to settle in when they first came to England. Arriving from Portugal, there was only one place to head for.

Liverpool, who have won the English top-flight league title 20 times.

Liverpool, who have won eight FA Cups, 10 League Cups, and 16 FA Community Shields.

He knows all the statistics. If there was an exam in Liverpool's club history he would pass it with his eyes closed. He knows all the players, even the ones from years ago, long before he was born.

More impressive than all of the national competitions is the fact that the club has won the European Cup – now the Champions League – a grand total of six times, the most for any English club in history. They've also won the Europa League three times. They are, quite simply, the best team in Europe.

He'd give anything to be able to watch another match with his dad.

He wishes his dad was here for lots of other reasons, too. Not just football or for Andre starting secondary school.

If his dad was still here, it would make his mum less sad, for one thing. And he wouldn't have to do so much around the house if his father was still here to help.

Even though it's more than four years since Duarte left, the boy has been thinking about his father more than ever lately. Perhaps it's because he is about to become a teenager. There are lots of things that are confusing at the moment. He has no one to ask the things that boys should be able to ask their fathers about.

So much has changed since the summer of 2020, which he remembers as the worst year of his life. Duarte left their family during lockdown, in the middle of the pandemic. He went back to Portugal, leaving the boy and the rest of the family that he brought to England behind.

It seems like a long time ago now. So long that he sometimes has to look at the photo albums in the sitting room to properly remember what his dad looks like.

Sometimes he blames his father for what happened. Sometimes he blames the pandemic. Sometimes he blames Tomas, but he knows that isn't fair: Tomas was only a baby. He didn't ask to be born. Sometimes he thinks it's just that the world isn't fair.

His father had been working for a building firm, making good money. But when lockdown happened and Covid smothered the world, the work stopped suddenly. Duarte didn't qualify for 'furlough' because he didn't have a contract, so he was just laid off.

When they had to stand in the spaced-out lines waiting to buy food in supermarkets they were spat at. Duarte said that the spitting was because they were Portuguese, and it had started because of Brexit. That made him sad.

His father, in particular, had loved being in Britain – so much so that he always insisted they call him Dad, rather than Papai.

There was a madness in lockdown, he said. People became paranoid and small-minded. They closed-in against outsiders.

It wasn't just strangers in queues. They were even ignored by people who had spoken to them before and used to be friendly.

And so, with no work and no money, and six mouths to feed, his dad went back home to Portugal.

He said he was going to stay with the boy's grandmother, Vovó, so he could find work. The boy had been with his father to visit Vovó the summer before, on a holiday. So when his father first left for Portugal, claiming that he was a stranded citizen who needed to be repatriated after the aeroplanes were grounded and most travel was stopped for months, they all thought at first that it would be a kind of holiday. That it wouldn't be forever.

Duarte told them that it would only be for a short time. That he would see them all – the boy, his brothers, and their mother, Eliana – very soon.

'I have to go. Vovó needs me because of the pandemic. And anyway, there is no work here. But if I am in Portugal, I can earn enough money to send back to my family here in Liverpool. Just until things get back to normal.'

They waved him off without realising.

He never came back.

The money never came.

Nothing was ever normal again.

The boy isn't really sure what normal is anymore. They have been struggling ever since. It has become normal not to have enough to eat and to have to go to the foodbank. It is normal not to have enough money to keep the house warm in winter. It is normal for the boy to have to look after his little brothers.

Occasionally, he feels that it's all his fault. Sometimes that's a simpler answer than blaming lockdown.

The way Duarte said goodbye when he left, telling the boy that he was *the man* while Duarte was gone had made him feel very proud and grown up at the time. After all, it was a big responsibility.

But being the man is hard when you have to do it all of the time. Still, he has made a promise and he will keep it. He won't let his dad down.

Tomas, the youngest of the brothers, had only just been born when Duarte left.

Now he keeps wondering if Duarte knew when he left that he would not be returning to them. It feels as if his dad was running away. But how could you leave a tiny baby like that and not come back?

'Why don't we go to Portugal and find Dad?' he sometimes asked his mother during those long lockdown months when there was no school.

'Because,' Eliana said.

And nothing ever followed 'because'. It was as if the word had a full stop at the end of it. He remembers that, particularly, because school had sent some worksheets home at the start of lockdown and he'd had to practise full stops. Full stops ended a sentence. 'Because' was the end of her sentence and it was final. Duarte was never coming back.

It's getting later. He knows he should get up, get out of bed, get his brothers up and start the day. All of these thoughts that often come in the morning aren't helpful. He tries to push them away. He hates thinking about lockdown, because it is the time when everything went wrong. Before lockdown they'd been happy. A proper family.

Then they weren't.

His mum says that Duarte's sadness was depression. She knows, she says, because she had it too, after Tomas was born.

Eliana was supposed to keep working during lockdown. She worked as a cleaner in a supermarket, which made her a 'key worker'. Duarte stayed at home with the boys while Eliana went out to work and did long shifts. But after Duarte left, she couldn't leave the children because there was no one to leave them with. Especially Tomas, who was too small and who cried a lot.

He wonders what they could have done differently to make his dad stay. Whether there was something he could have said. If he could have behaved differently. Done more.

Or whether, once Duarte had left, they could have tried harder to make him come back. But these are old thoughts that go round and round and round inside his head. He really must get up and get going now, or they will be late for school. It is down to him these days.

He heard his mum talking to her friend, Maria, late at night, some months after his dad had gone. They opened a bottle of wine together and as they got nearer to the bottom of it, the words got louder and drifted up the stairs. It was a conversation he knew he was not meant to hear. 'Because' was *not* the end of the sentence. Eliana *had* tried to find Duarte.

'He seems to have forgotten that he even had a family. He has become a different person. I don't know him. He won't speak to me. He won't speak to the children.'

The boy thinks that, if only he could get himself to Portugal, he might be able to make his dad remember them all.

'I was a good woman,' his mum told Maria. 'A good wife.'

'There is no doubt about that,' Maria assured her.

'I gave him sons.'

'And very good boys they are,' Maria said. 'You should be proud of them.'

'I was patient. He said he needed time. I have tried to give him time. But there is no more time.'

'It wasn't you,' Maria's voice was soothing. 'You weren't to blame.'

'I don't want to be here anymore. Not in this place. This is the place that broke him. Duarte was heartbroken by the way his old colleagues and people in the community treated him. They stole his dignity, they broke his heart.'

'It was a difficult time. People can be so cruel.'

'Why, Maria?' Eliana was crying by now. 'Why did the people turn on us like that? We worked hard at our jobs and joined in with the community. We always knew, from when we first came, that we must join in. People from other countries who come to England are not always treated well, or made to feel welcome. But we made sure that we made friends.'

'You did that,' Maria agreed.

'It was lockdown that did it,' Eliana cried. 'When lockdown came they all betrayed us. Duarte couldn't cope with it. He felt nothing but betrayal and despair. Men who had previously been his friend on the building sites were cruel to him, and to other people who had come to England to work. He had been a good worker in Portugal, he ran building sites, he worked directly with the architects and engineers. But in England he was a – how do you say it? A skivvy.'

Eliana has also tried talking to Vovó, she told Maria. 'But mothers believe their sons and she believes a new story: that I wasn't a good wife. That I am a slut and I am lazy, and I was mean to Duarte. She thinks I was mean to her son.'

The boy didn't know back then what a slut was, just that it was a bad word. He had been shocked to hear his mother using bad words.

'There's no way back. Now both my husband and my mother-in-law have stopped communicating with me. It's as if I don't exist. I've been shut out. Worse, my own family who live close to my husband's mother have also begun to back away. In our little village, people believe the men, not the women. And I am not there to defend myself.'

'Don't speak like that, Eliana. You are a good wife and a good mother.'

The boy wondered if that was true. If it *was* really true, would his dad have left them?

II

Having walked his brothers to their school, the boy now legs it up the road to his own school. Even though it's cloudy, the day is warm but they have to wear blazers, regardless of the temperature. It's a stupid rule.

These days, he isn't as naive as he was back then, when his dad first left. He's grown up a lot. He has come to know that some of the things his mum said are true: people are mean.

At school, he has regularly been on the receiving end of negative rants and verbal abuse. It didn't happen in primary school, but almost as soon as he started secondary school he was singled out. 'Pork and Cheese' (not Portuguese) is a favourite taunt of Ollie, a boy in his year, who also regularly tells him to, 'Fuck off back to where you came from.'

It's a cruel thing to say, because he doesn't even remember living in Portugal. He was only two years old when he came to the UK. 'Get back on your boat,' is another classic. But they never came by boat. Duarte brought his family to the UK on an aeroplane; he can just about remember it, or perhaps he thinks he does because of the photographs. So 'get back on your boat' is just dumb. It doesn't make any sense. But when he shouted that at Ollie, back in Year 7, everyone laughed and it just made everything worse.

So now he tries to ignore the shitty jibes and keeps himself to himself. But it makes him worry for Andre and what will happen to him in September when he starts at the school. Primary school is like a little bubble, but everything changes after that. The bullying is way worse. He knows he'll have to protect Andre. But that is nothing new. He has been looking after his brothers since lockdown.

Being the man of the house, just like his dad made him promise.

He used to tell his mum what was going on, but it only made her more upset, so he doesn't say anything now.

'Racism is a terrible thing,' Eliana says. 'And it doesn't make sense. I don't understand it. I don't understand why some people here don't see the expats that live in Spain as migrants. So it's fine for them to have houses in another country? Or all of those British kids who settle in Australia after travelling and doing bar work and other low paid jobs. How is that different?'

The boy doesn't know how it's different and he doesn't

answer when his mum starts on one of these rants. She always says the same thing.

'Portugal is part of the Western World. British people own holiday homes there just like they do in Spain. They want the beaches and the wine. So why do white people target us here, even though they all want to go brown when they're on holiday? They come to Portugal to get as dark as the Portuguese. They love it if they are mistaken for a local. But they still despise us. It makes no sense! Over here they treat us Portuguese with contempt. And we have done nothing to deserve it.'

The boy already knows this to be true.

His mum took all of the hurt to heart, and she needed to find a way to numb it. It started with wine. The odd glass here and there. Nights like the one where his mum poured out her heart to Maria and didn't realise he was listening. Then it moved from nights to days, and then from wine to vodka. Lately, she has stopped getting out of bed in the morning. The boy has had to do more than just feed his brothers and do the school drop-offs and pick-ups. As hard as Eliana tried to keep it going after his father left, now it's almost like she is disappearing as a mother. She is disappearing into herself. Disappearing into the sofa that she rarely moves from. Disappearing into a vodka bottle.

Running up the road in the heat has made him break into a sweat. He loves the sun, but he hasn't seen much of it so far this year. He seems to spend so much time looking after his brothers and his mum. He stands outside the school entrance and presses the buzzer to come in. He can see his own reflection in the glass. His nose is too big for his face. He has spots on his forehead and chin, and his duckdown facial hair shows up on his putty-coloured skin. He scowls; he thinks he looks disgusting. Perhaps, when he finally reaches being a teenager, he'll turn from the ugly duckling into the swan.

Mr Piggott walks up to the door to release the lock and allow him in.

'Late again, I see,' he says, with a frown.

The boy mutters an apology and lowers his head.

This lateness is everything his 'old' parents would have hated.

'I'm sorry, I didn't catch that,' Mr Piggott says.

He makes his soft voice go up a notch. 'I said, I'm sorry, Sir.'

Mr Piggott usually just lets him through with a shake of his head and a reminder about the importance of punctuality, but today he stops and asks him why he is late so often. 'Perhaps you need a detention to help you remember to be on time. We don't want it to become a habit, do we?'

He keeps his head down. 'I'm sorry, Sir. I was late this morning because I have to take my brothers to school.'

Mr Piggott frowns again. 'Why is that your job? It's no good if it starts interfering with your education. What about your mum or dad? Why don't they take your brothers?'

The boy shifts from foot to foot. He doesn't know where to put himself. He can't answer the question honestly without bringing shame. But neither can he lie. And he can't have a detention. Not an after-school one, anyway. He needs to be able to collect his brothers.

'My dad left in lockdown, Sir, and my mum–'. He pauses to choose a word. 'My mum is not very well at the moment.'

His face burns with embarrassment. He can feel his cheeks getting hotter. He dares a quick glance up at Mr Piggott.

The teacher's voice has softened a little. 'Sorry to hear that, I wasn't aware of your family circumstances.'

The boy nods, desperately wanting this humiliating conversation to be over.

'Well, quickly sign in and get straight off to lessons. Let's not waste any more of the day. And I hope your mother gets well soon.'

So does the boy, although the idea of his mum recovering seems remote to him.

'Yes, Sir, thank you, Sir.'

He signs the late book, noticing his name appears in

several places over the last few days. If he gets up earlier, he could get his brothers to school quicker and stop himself from being late. But they don't always open the gates of the primary school right on time, and his own timings are very tight in the mornings. Plus, Tomas takes an age to get ready and can never find his shoes. They need better systems at home to make it work. He tries to be organised, but it's hard being organised for everyone.

He looks up at the clock to work out where he should be, then walks, as fast as he can without running, in the direction of his form room. There's still a few minutes to go of registration time with his tutor before the first period of the day starts.

Another member of staff, whose name he doesn't know, calls out, 'You there! Laces! Do up your laces!' She isn't a regular teacher, maybe a teaching assistant, but she seems to enjoy her little bit of authority. She has told him off before. She is one of those types who seems to pick holes in all the students as they walk past. Some adults are like that. Nothing is ever good enough. She could find fault however neat your uniform is. But he will not be rude and answer back, like some of the other kids in his year would.

He looks down to his feet. It's the lace on the shoe of his right foot which has come undone. He deliberately keeps his laces quite loose to make the shoes a little bit more comfortable. His feet hurt because the shoes are really too small for him now. There isn't any money for new shoes, so they will have to do for the time being.

He bends down to tie them up as instructed, and as he does so, the heavy rucksack, with all his books for the six periods of the day, slides down from his back and whacks him in the face.

He closes his eyes. 'I hate my life,' he mutters, to no one in particular. Because no one is listening.

It's one of those days when the universe seems set against him.

That extra little interaction means that now he's too late for form time. The bell goes and students start to spill out into corridors, so he joins the throng and heads in the other direction, towards the science block, ready for chemistry. It could be worse. He quite likes chemistry. Not the subject, particularly, but because the seating plan allows him to sit near his one proper friend, Jamie. He's been friends with Jamie since primary school, but since they made all their option choices, they are apart for most of their lessons.

Once upon a time, he'd go to Jamie's house after school to play and have tea. Jamie has a nice house: neat and tidy and clean. Easier when you have both parents around. But they've kind of grown out of it. He hasn't been there for ages. He can't, really. Not anymore. His life has become too busy for hanging out and doing not very much. But Jamie's sound, and they are still good friends in school. He's never gone into detail about his home situation, but Jamie gets it. Today Jamie doesn't take the piss when a huge hunger growl escapes from his tummy, even though Jamie is sitting right next to him and must have heard, because it comes during a quiet bit of the lesson, when they are in the middle of doing a short test on atomic structure and the whole class is writing in silence.

Instead, at breaktime, Jamie doesn't ask him, but just goes ahead and buys two baguettes plus crisps and a drink when they go to the canteen. Jamie pushes the baguette across the table towards him, then opens the packet of crisps fully, so it's like a silver plate to share between them.

'Thanks, mate. I can't pay you back at the moment.'

'No need. I don't want you to.'

They both know that 'at the moment' means nothing. He's not going to be able to pay Jamie back – ever.

Most days, he manages to find something to bring with him from home to eat at school, but this week the cupboards are bare. His mum hasn't put any money into his school account, accessed via each pupil's thumbprint, since the first week of term in Year 7. There's no money, but even if there was, she doesn't like doing anything online. That was the kind of stuff that his dad used to take care of. And anyway, she is in such a deep depression – or alcoholic haze, he isn't sure which – that she has probably forgotten all the passwords. So no, he won't be buying Jamie a baguette back anytime soon.

His younger brothers get free school lunches. Which guarantees them a decent meal every day. Thank God, as there's no way he could make packed lunches for all of them every morning. There wouldn't be enough time or food.

He had to sort their free lunches out though. He had to go and be 'the man'. He stood in reception at the primary school, waiting in line with the other parents at the start of the term, so that he could talk to the admin lady about adding his brothers to the list. The receptionist had done it for them the previous term, too. He has no idea about paperwork or any of that. The other parents bring in forms. But she told him not to worry and somehow it gets done – and it means at least they get a good meal at lunchtime and don't go hungry.

It's a bit more difficult to organise it for himself, though. At the secondary school they don't just take his word for it, like they do at the primary school. 'We'll need to speak to your mum,' was all they said. But she won't speak to them. It's too embarrassing to take it further. Humiliating to have to explain that he and his family can't afford to eat properly. Easier just to go hungry. Look at Mr Piggott this morning, who didn't know anything about his family situation. But why should he? It's a big school and he isn't the only one who struggles. Everyone has their problems. Not just him. Lots of kids are living hand to mouth like he is. Most of the teachers don't seem to recognise what's going on, or, if they do, they seem to blame the student for their situation, looking down on the kids like him who struggle to pay their way, or find the right school uniform they need.

It's supposed to be a good school. One of the better ones in the area. It has a good reputation. In assemblies, all they go on about is the importance of exam results. The school has high academic expectations for its students, which is a good thing. He wants to do well too. But the area they're in is mostly poor and many families suffer. It's just a fact. They've looked at the history of Liverpool in their lessons: how it was a major port during the 18th century, wealthy because it was part of the transatlantic slave trade, and then a central city in the Industrial Revolution. During its heyday in the 19th century, they built iconic structures, like the Royal Albert Dock. But then it went into a decline.

There was supposed to be another upshift when Liverpool was named as European Capital of Culture in the early 2000s, but not anymore. Now Liverpool isn't even in Europe as far as some people are concerned, and it's all about austerity measures instead. You couldn't live here and not know about the challenges related to deindustrialisation and the decline of its docks. His father wasn't the only one to lose his job and suffer economic hardship because of the pandemic. There are plenty of other kids in the same boat as him. He needs to suck it up.

But every school day feels stressful.

And he is so tired. Sometimes it feels as if he has the responsibilities of a boy, a father *and* a mother. But he's trying to do it all without the resources that a father or a mother would have. He has no money or access to any – and no real voice.

Because they've no food in, he'll have to go to the foodbank after school. There are a number of foodbanks around his area that are run through churches or community hubs, but there's one big one that he likes to visit. It's a slightly longer walk, but the volunteers know him and his brothers and always seem pleased to see them. It's mostly older ladies who volunteer there, and they're good at helping him pick out things that will be easy to cook or will go far in a large family. Sometimes they keep stuff by, under the counter or out the back, especially for him. They're kind and give his brothers something to play with, or keep them distracted while he goes round choosing things and, at the end, they help him load up his bags.

It's not so bad. In some ways, it's actually nicer than going to an ordinary shop. You're meant to be allowed a certain number of items, but they always let him have a bit more. And it's easier not to have to do all the maths. When he goes to the supermarket for things they can't get at the foodbank, he has to do a lot of calculations to make sure he has enough money to cover what's in his basket when he gets to the checkout. Otherwise it's really shaming if he has to get round the queuing people behind him to put something back.

He collects his brothers from school. Andre has them lined up, waiting to go. You're supposed to wait in your class line until a parent arrives, but they've been pretty good about letting Andre wait with the little ones until he gets there.

There are rich pickings at the foodbank today: large packets of cereal that his brothers like, lots of bread and pasta. They also have some pastries that they can eat on the way home. You never know exactly what you will be able to get, but today's a day where there is plenty.

The community foodbank also has a separate area with clothes and shoes, in a little room to the side of the main food bit.

'Ah, Mr Pereira, come into my emporium,' one of the ladies calls out.

He doesn't know what an 'emporium' is, but the boys follow her to the side room and he likes it. It's decked out like a proper clothes shop, with shelves and clothing rails. There are used and unused shoes, trainers and school uniforms on one side. But all sorts of other stuff, too like sports clothes and football kits. They can't be giving all this stuff away. It's too good. He feels embarrassed – and ashamed. He hates this feeling of shame. It never goes away, no matter how used to it he gets. He wants the new stuff, but he wants to be able to offer some money to contribute towards it and he can't. He has taken on the role of head of the household without a penny to his name.

'Don't be shy,' the lady says. She is soon joined by another volunteer who is just as insistent.

'Boys, you take what you need. Let's help you get some new shoes.'

His feet are hurting from the too-small shoes, and so must his brothers' be. They are all growing so fast and school shoes are expensive.

His brothers look at him expectantly for confirmation. He gives them a nod, so that they know it's okay to do as the ladies say.

They sit on the floor in a row while the ladies bring shoes to them.

His own feet are hot and sweaty and he feels uncomfortable having anyone near them, especially when he takes his shoes off to reveal the holes in his socks. His brothers' feet are in the same state. But the ladies don't seem fazed by this and slip on different shoes for size until they find shoes that fit each of the boys. Once they are kitted out with school shoes, they start the search for trainers. Not just trainers. He spots a pair of football boots in size nine, his size! He picks them up. The lady sees him and nods. She looks in another box and pulls out a pair of football socks.

'Take them.'

'Are you sure?'

'Absolutely. 100%. They are yours.'

This is brilliant. And he has an idea. He's been worried about how to get Andre the new uniform that he'll need for September. Perhaps now is his best chance. He finds himself telling the lady that Andre will be starting at the new school after the holidays.

'In which case, he'll need some uniform, won't he?'

They find a blazer in the right size, some school trousers, two polo shirts and some PE kit. Most of it is new. His mum will be really pleased that Andre is sorted for September.

'Result!' he says. 'That is an absolute touch.'

Andre looks very happy kitted out in his new gear.

'Just don't go growing over the summer!' he tells his brother.

The boys stagger out of the place with so much stuff they can barely carry it all, but no one is complaining. He takes the heavy bags with tins, and Andre and Dinis carry the other bags of food and drink between them. They manage to stuff some of the clothes and trainers into their now-bulging school bags. Tomas takes a carrier bag with his new shoes in.

They have to stop a few times on the way home, so that he can change hands and redistribute the weight.

'Can't wait to show Mum,' Andre says.

Dinis is too overwhelmed to speak, but the smile on his face says it all.

When they walk through the front door, they pass the door to the room where Eliana sits, staring out of the window.

'Come and look,' he calls out, as the four of them trip straight through into the kitchen to spill their hoard out onto the kitchen counter. 'We've done the shopping and we've got new stuff to wear!'

There's no answer from his mum.

Tomas races in to show her his new trainers.

'Mama!' he calls, running over to her. 'Look what they had at the foodbank!' He scrambles up into her lap. 'Do you like them?'

The boy stands in the doorway, as if watching a scene in a film. Eliana is still staring through the window but without seeming to focus on anything in particular. She is distracted. It is like part of her has upped and gone.

'Mama,' Tomas calls again, desperate for her attention. 'You're not looking.'

'Very nice,' Eliana says, eventually.

She places her hand on Tomas's back and her youngest child curls up there and sucks his thumb.

Perhaps she is getting better, he thinks, as he watches them from the doorway. He hasn't seen Tomas snuggle up to her like that for a while. Or at least, he hasn't seen Eliana respond when he does. Perhaps things can change again. He remembers how she used to be so affectionate with them all. He's too old for that sort of thing now, of course – too grown up for cuddles – but his brothers should have it.

'They're very smart trainers,' she whispers, but she doesn't smile.

They take it in turns to do a bit of a fashion parade for Eliana, then take their clothes upstairs to put them away. Her lack of enthusiasm doesn't dull their own.

The boy strokes his football boots. They might be the most beautiful thing he has ever seen. When it's time for bed, he puts them next to his pillow, so that he can sleep beside them tonight.

He dreams of football. Of playing matches with his father watching from the sidelines, cheering him on. Of scoring the winner in the cup final.

All in his new boots.

III

On the 3rd of July, news reports of the death of Liverpool F.C.'s Diogo Jota begin to circulate. The city goes into mourning, and so does their household.

Andre persuades him to set up a shrine to their footballing hero in their bedroom. They find a picture, light a candle and arrange some flowers around it.

'Do you think we could talk to Dad?' Dinas asks. 'He'll be sad, too.'

They try to phone, but don't get him. All of the boys are devastated by the loss. Jota is such a hero. To be killed, so tragically, alongside his brother in a car crash. It feels like such a waste. The boy is heartbroken once again. He has lost their dad overseas, his mama to vodka and depression, and now his hero.

They light the candle every day through the summer holidays and into the new term.

Their mother drinks even more.

'It's the last straw,' she weeps. 'His presence here in the city helped the community. It's a tragedy.'

The boy prepares tea and calls the younger ones down. Tonight he has cooked potatoes, beans and fish fingers. Meals are determined, more than ever, by what the foodbank has to offer.

The volunteers at the foodbank have been good at giving them extra stuff each time he goes, which is a good job, because it was hard to do lunch as well as breakfast and dinner every day over the summer holidays and there's no more money.

All the money goes on those damn bottles that his mother buys, the ones that the boy hates so much.

The new term starts, and there is still a bit of heat in the sun, maybe more than usual for this time of year; September has stayed fine, so far, and autumn hasn't kicked in properly yet.

For now, they can keep the kitchen back door open in the evenings. The room is too small to have a table, but they arrange themselves on the doorstep and around the end of the kitchen counter to eat. Andre looks good in his smart new uniform, and has survived his first week of big school relatively unscathed.

It was almost a relief to get back to school for the new term. It's been lonely. He hasn't seen Jamie at all over the summer holidays. He couldn't, he was too busy trying to look after his brothers. The summer seemed to go on forever. And his mama has been getting worse as each week passes. She has taken to getting up later and later in the day – if she makes it into her bed at all.

She doesn't *do* anything other than watch television and sip from her bottle.

Her world has shrunk to nothing. She seems to move between the couch and her bed, staying in her pyjamas until after lunch and finally getting dressed in the late afternoon, when she drags herself out and walks up to the shop for her next bottle of vodka.

She is very, very unhappy.

It has been a long time since she smiled. Her mouth seems to have set in a hard line. He remembers how much his mama used to smile – all the time – when he was younger. She would tell him and his brothers how beautiful and clever they were. But that was before, back in the days when his dad was still around.

She would make them delicious meals. Not beans and fish fingers, but proper Portuguese food: bacalhau, sardines, and duck rice. She'd bake cakes, biscuits, and treats. Another thing she hasn't done for a long, long time.

When his mother had been baking and it was a nice day, they would take a picnic over to the fields. His father would carry the hamper that his mother had carefully packed. The boy would give anything to be able to taste one of those freshly-baked custard tarts she used to make. Before and after the meal, they would all play football together.

He'd love to be able to rewind time and return to the family they were before Covid and lockdown. Before he knew about being called 'Pork and Cheese'. Before everything was bloody ruined.

He has pretty much taken over all of the cooking now. And he isn't very good at it. Stupidly, he feels a tear sliding down his cheek and wipes it away with the back of his sleeve, fast, before anyone else sees it. He doesn't mean to cry. He's too old for tears. But he feels so sorry for himself, he can't stop it.

The world doesn't make any sense now. But there is no point in trying to think about it too much. And there's no point in feeling sorry for himself. He just has to get on with it.

He takes a plate of the bland food to his mother.

She nods her thanks and puts the plate on her lap, but makes no move to eat it.

'Mama, eat.'

She looks up at him. He notices that she looks even more tired and old than she usually does. She isn't really that old, but she looks like an old woman. Her hair is dull. He remembers it being thick and shiny when he was little. Her skin looks grey. She is just a mass of sadness.

'Come on, I made it for you. You need to eat something. Please.'

Eliana sighs and sits up straighter in the chair. It takes her an enormous amount of effort. The cutlery hovers over the food for a moment, until the knife and fork land, almost of their own accord, somewhere on the plate.

'Go on.'

She stares at the food on the fork.

'Go on. We don't want to waste it.'

It is like trying to get Tomas to eat when he was tiny. He tries to be patient. He is aware that he sounds like the adult, and his mama is the child.

The fork reaches her mouth and he watches her swallow the food.

'Thank you, Mama.'

She smiles a weak smile. This is good, he thinks. A smile. Hold on to it.

'Again.'

After a few more mouthfuls she sits back with the plate still in her lap. 'I'll have some more in a minute.'

But he's satisfied. For now. A morsel or two is better than nothing. He leaves her to it, and returns to his brothers in the kitchen.

By the time he gets there, the other boys have more or less finished their plates. But they know the routine and they all help him wash up and clear away, even Tomas, who always does the cutlery. Necessity means that they are well trained now.

Homework has kicked in with a vengeance now that the new term has begun, but it can wait for a bit. He's trying to organise some routine and structure into their days. The time straight after dinner is free time. Because the weather is so nice, they go out into their little garden and play a game with a bit of broken fence panel and an old tennis ball. It's a strange version of French cricket that they've invented between them, with different scores for different targets hit with the ball. The fence is one, the tree trunk is four, the table on its side, like a target, is six. Once, Eliana might have joined in. Not any more.

After an hour or so of play, he settles his brothers down to do their homework. It's boring, but it needs to be done. This is what his dad used to do. His dad would ask him how lessons had gone and what he'd learned that day, so he does the same to his brothers.

'And what was the best thing that happened at school today?' He uses the same tone as his dad used to do with him.

He tries to think about the best thing that happened in his own day, because focusing on the good stuff helps. The best thing about today was that he had a PE lesson, one of his option subjects, and discovered that Ollie isn't in the group. Ollie, who leads the Pork and Cheese taunts, is still in his tutor group, but not in so many of his subject classes now that they've moved into Year 9.

He goes through the homework, reads with Tomas and writes in Tomas's reading log, before packing up his book bag for the morning. Dinis is allowed to write in his own reading log these days, and Andre no longer has one now that he has switched schools. He also doesn't have much homework to do.

'Don't worry, you will,' he warns his brother. 'They go easy on the Year 7s for the first couple of weeks. Then they'll cook you. '

The house is a mess. It's a state. Even though they all help to clear up, it's never properly clean. Not clean that you'd want to invite anyone into. He can't do it all. It's very hard when his mama sits on the sofa all day. He can't be both parents at the same time. He isn't even up to being a replacement for one.

He goes to collect his mama's plate. She hasn't eaten any more, in spite of her promise. Instead, she pours herself another drink. He wishes she wouldn't. Her eyes are red and watery. He doesn't know if that's from tears or tiredness, but either way he knows it's made worse by the vodka.

He sits in the room with her.

'The boys have done their homework.'

She smiles at him. 'You are a good boy. You are such a good son. I don't know what I'd do without you.'

He nods and thanks her.

'But I really can't do this anymore,' she follows up with 'I don't want to be here. I don't want to stay in this place.'

He feels like he might be sick. He doesn't know what she means by 'this place'. Does she mean here in the house, or here in Liverpool, or here in the world? Is his mother actually telling him that she wants to die?

'Don't talk like that, Mama.'

He swallows and fetches the photo album from the shelf. 'Here.'

She likes to look at the photo album. Though the downside is it always makes her cry. There are pictures of her as a girl, younger than he is now. Sometimes it's hard to believe the little girl in the photographs has become his mama. He sits down beside her, moving closer as she turns the pages slowly. She smells sour, but he forces himself not to react.

He stares at the pictures, even though he's seen them hundreds of times before. She looks very happy, different to how she is now. Everything looks different in them. The colours are slightly strange, as if the world itself was a different place back then.

He tries to keep track of which ones provoke the most reaction, which ones are making her smile. Sometimes he catches her eye and they share a moment of recognition.

She sighs. 'I hate what I have become.'

He wants to say, *then stop it. Stop drinking. Go back to how you were.* But he doesn't speak.

His parents were so young when they met. They were children together at school. There are a couple of pictures of them with their families, all together. His grandparents. There is a posed wedding photograph. The wedding was in their village in Portugal, and there are more photos of them together outside the church and beneath the trees.

They look like a couple in a film, smiling and in love. His dad was very good-looking. He still hopes that once all this acne clears and his face isn't so shiny, he might look more like his dad.

'Oh, my son. I hate this. I hate this country. It's destroyed my marriage. It has sunk us into poverty. It wasn't his fault. Your father was a good man. Duarte was a kind man and these people broke his heart.'

'He left us,' the boy whispers.

'Because he had to get away. It wasn't just his construction job that suffered. All of the companies, hotels, catering, agriculture, all of it. The NHS. They all took a huge hit when the foreigners left for their home countries. The biggest sadness, really, is that he came here to give us – his family – a better life and ended up being pushed out. I tell you, son, all I want is to gather enough money to go back home, to take my boys back home. To live again with my family.'

'One day, Mama.'

'It's not possible. My family thinks I am an alcoholic. I *am* drinking a bit too much, I know it. But it's the only thing that gives me any peace. I want to lift myself up again and take care of you all again. I really do. I want that more than anything.'

'So do I.' The words stick in his throat, because those stupid tears are threatening to come again and he will not let his mama see him cry.

'My mama and my Vovó worked so hard to give me and my sisters everything we needed,' she says. 'I'm sorry I haven't been able to do the same. I'm sorry that I couldn't buy you the clothes, and the shoes, and the trainers. It should be me buying you those things, not a charity.'

'It's okay, Mama.'

'I have failed you.'

'No, Mama.'

'I have. You deserve more. Much, much more than this.'

The tears that he wants to cry are falling down his mama's cheeks.

'My glass is empty. Fetch me another drink, son.'

He hesitates for a moment, but it is so hard to say no to her.

IV

The September sun is very hot today. It feels as if the back of his head is burning as he waits with Andre, standing outside Tomas' classroom, after school. Dinis knows to gather there too when he comes out of class.

Usually Tomas runs over when he sees his brother, but today Tomas's teacher walks with him towards them instead.

'Hello there, you must be Tomas' big brothers. Do you have time to have a chat today?'

Uh-oh. He doesn't want to talk to her, but he must, in case something is wrong with Tomas at school. He nods.

'Come over to my classroom. I don't want everyone to hear.'

'My brother–' he gestures to the other lines of pupils walking out to the playground, where Dinis will appear any minute.

'He can come too, don't worry. And Andre.'

Tomas' teacher is called Mrs Graham and has been at the school for a couple of years. She taught Andre when he was in Year 4. She is very nice and makes sure that the younger boys are all settled on the reading mat with books to look at. 'Maybe you can read to them, Andre,' she suggests, before turning her attention back to the conversation.

'Have a seat.'

They head towards one of the classroom tables on the other side of the room, away from the boys, so that they won't be easily overheard and can have their conversation in private.

Uh-oh, he thinks again. Something must be very wrong, even though Mrs Graham is still smiling. He pulls out a chair. He remembers these small chairs from when he was a pupil here himself. But he doesn't remember them being so absurdly tiny. He supposes that they must have been. They haven't shrunk. It just shows how much he has grown since he was last here. How much he has become the man now.

'Really, I'd like to speak with your parents, but I know that they don't come to the school. It's great that you're able to drop them off and pick them up each day, but I have to ask: is everything else okay at home?'

He doesn't know what to say. How is he supposed to answer that question? He doesn't want outsiders knowing their business. He is proud, just like his dad used to be. Besides, his mama wouldn't want him to say anything bad about the family, anything shameful about their home. Anything that might bring strangers in to see the state of their lives.

But at the same time, he is not coping. None of them are coping.

He shrugs his shoulders. It is the only response he can think to give without being untruthful.

He hopes that Mrs Graham won't think he is being rude, but he really doesn't want to have this conversation. He tries to stand up. He knows that if he says 'no', and lets her know that they are not coping, it will feel like a failure. It will feel like betrayal. It would be embarrassing to say that his mama isn't looking after them. He doesn't want his mama to fail, or to get into any trouble. Besides, he's doing a good job of sorting everything out. As he tries to rise, he is wedged in by the little chair. He drops back down.

The teacher says, 'Look, I'll get straight to it. I don't know what's going on, but I've noticed that Tomas has some hygiene issues.'

Mrs Graham says the words kindly, but he is mortified. 'He's beginning to smell a little. I don't want the other children to notice. He needs to have more baths and to wear clean underpants.'

This is terrible. He has been so busy worrying about Andre at the new school and making sure that they all have food, that he hasn't thought about this.

'He's five years old now, but I've noticed that he still has a few issues with going to the toilet.'

Mrs Graham hands him a clear plastic bag. Inside is a pair of pants. He can see by the moisture on the plastic that they are wet.

'Don't worry, they're not dirty. I've rinsed them out and we've put him in some clean pants, but his bottom is sore from where he has been wetting himself. Here's some cream you can use. It's a new tube, don't worry. No one else has used it but, if you can put this on his bottom, on the red sore area after a wash, it will help soothe him and make sure that he isn't too uncomfortable to sit still in class.'

If Tomas is doing this at home, too, then he has kept it quiet. Like all of them, Tomas is just trying to cope and get on with it quietly.

'It's because he isn't properly toilet-trained. But it can be very easily sorted out, don't worry.' She nods.

Mrs Graham keeps telling him not to worry, but he *is* worried. How could he not be? And horrified. And embarrassed. And ashamed. There's always so much shame. He should have thought more about this: about the routine of baths and about washing lots of pants for Tomas and about checking when he's been to the toilet.

'I'm sorry,' he says, without looking at her. He doesn't want to look her in the eye. The shame of it all.

'There's nothing to be sorry for. It's not your fault. It's just one of those things. We just need to sort it. Now, I have here a packet of new pants that you can have for Tomas. Okay? There are eight pairs in there and I think they're the right size for him.'

He takes the new pants. 'Thank you.'

'And you can talk to me at the end of any school day and tell me if you think there is anything else he needs.'

He nods, but doesn't trust himself to speak. Why do these tears insist on coming when he doesn't want them to? A man wouldn't cry like this.

He blinks them away and takes a deep breath. People are very kind. The ladies at the foodbank. This teacher. Mrs Graham is a nice lady. He is very relieved that she isn't cross, she isn't punishing him and hasn't said anything about telling anyone else.

'Thank you,' he manages, eventually. 'Thank you for not–'

'No problem.' She smiles at him. 'You're a very good big brother. You're doing a great job. He's lucky to have you.'

On the way home, he tells Andre not to worry when Andre asks what the conversation with the teacher was all about. But he is absolutely furious with himself for not looking after Tomas better. He will use the cream, as she has suggested, and he will check his brother's pants. He will make sure that Tomas is okay. He will check on how he is going to the toilet. He will not be needing Tomas's teacher, nice as she is, to have any more conversations like this with him.

When they get back, the first thing he does is go to check in on his mama. It should be her job to be checking these things for Tomas and making sure that he has clean pants every day, but of course she won't.

She is sitting in her chair with the TV on loud, as always.

'Hello, Mama.'

She doesn't take her eyes from the television, even though her eyes don't look like they are even focusing properly on whatever is on the screen. She gives a half nod to indicate that she has heard, but otherwise doesn't acknowledge their return. The almost-empty vodka bottle is in its usual position beside her.

No matter. He has things to do. He is going to be very busy tonight. First, dinner for the boys. He pulls tins of beans out of the cupboard and realises that he needs to get back down to the foodbank as soon as possible. There isn't much left in the cupboard. He digs around in the cupboard beneath the sink for washing powder.

He cooks tea for everyone: baked beans on toast, and a chopped up, cheap Swiss roll for pudding. Nice and easy.

'Time for a bath tonight,' he tells the boys. 'You run it

for Tomas and Dinis, Andre. Then bring down all of your uniforms for a wash.'

'I don't want to have a bath,' Tomas whines.

'Too bad, you're gettin' one,' he says, firmly. There is authority in his voice, naturally, after all this time of telling them what to do.

Tomas troops off after his brothers.

Now that he is aware of the smell of poo and sweat on them, he wonders why he couldn't smell it before. It's there, on the air. It permeates the house. It stays in his nostrils. He sniffs his own armpits, which are fine because he likes to shower, but the shirt itself is not, and he takes off his own clothes to add to the pile. They were washed over the summer, but not the blazer. How often are you supposed to wash a blazer? He hasn't thought about it before. He knows he needs clean polo shirts, but he hasn't given much consideration to the blazer. When did his mama last do this? He isn't sure. It's been a long time. He puts a wash on. He knows well enough how to use the machine. When it's done, he hangs it all out to dry on their fold-up washing line in the garden. The sun is still strong, so everything will easily be dry again for the morning, and fresh and clean.

He realises that his mama has also been in the same clothes for days. She smells the same as they do. Worse. That sour smell from the booze. And her hair looks really greasy. It could do with a wash – and that might make her feel better. When he goes to collect her plate after the beans on toast, he stands between her and the television so that she is forced to look at him.

'Mama, you need to wash and change your clothes today.' He uses the same firm tone that he did with his brothers.

She looks at him and holds out her arms for him to come forward. When he reaches her, she touches his face. 'Good boy. Yes, you're right. I will.'

He nods, then waits expectantly for her to move. He wants her to do it now. He has a burst of energy and he wants to get everything done. The bathroom is free, the other boys are all bathed and in their pyjamas, but she pauses.

'In a little while.'

He goes up to the bedrooms and sniffs the air. He can't remember the last time the sheets were washed. They don't smell too good either. Especially Tomas'. He must have been wetting the bed. He starts tugging at the sheets and pulling the duvet covers off to strip each bed down, including his mama's. The pillowcases are the worst. They look dirty and stained.

All the rooms smell bad. It's like he's just discovered a sense of smell. He opens the windows wide in all the rooms. He feels suddenly energised by the kindness of Tomas' teacher. He *can* do this. These things are not hard.

Mrs Graham has not shamed him, which she could have done. Instead she's been discreet and helped him.

The warmth of the long evening means that the polycotton sheets dry in next to no time. It takes two washes to fit it all in, but by the time the second wash is finished, the first load is almost dry. Putting all the sheets and pillowcases and duvet covers back on is harder, but he gets Andre to help.

He waits for the water to heat back up and then runs another bath for his mama.

'It's time now,' he insists. She must do it. She must listen to him. Things have to start changing around here. He won't take no for an answer. She wearily drags herself off of the sofa, half-smiling at him.

'And don't lock the door,' he warns. He wants her to leave it slightly ajar, in case she falls asleep in the water, as she has done before.

She is in there for a while, long enough for him to have a bit of a clear up in the sitting room. The spot where she sits has got saggy and stained. He hoovers all round the sofa, plumps up the cushions and wipes down the little side table with its sticky rings from glasses and cups.

In the morning, despite the bath, clean bed and fresh clothes, his mama is asleep in her chair with the vodka bottle and a glass beside her. She hasn't been to bed.

He knows that when they are out at school, she'll go

to Lidl to buy their cheapest vodka. This knowledge hurts him for more reasons than just knowing she's continuing to feed her habit. He wishes she would come home from there with food, or cakes, or anything for the boys, rather than just thinking about herself. It's hard knowing that the alcohol is more important to her than her sons.

He hates it.

And yet.

He still loves his mama. Still hopes that the next day will be different. Still believes that one day she will wake up better.

V

They swing by the community foodbank the following day after school. Andre waits outside with the younger boys while he goes round the tables and shelves collecting what he can.

Across the tables, he spots someone he knows: his mama's old friend, Maria. He hasn't seen her for a long time. Maria is someone he remembers from much happier days, when the Portuguese families would gather together in the cafés or in each other's houses. Maria sometimes worked in one of the Portuguese supermarkets that Eliana shopped in, the two women met there and became firm friends. But his mama has stopped going out, stopped seeing so many of her friends these days. Maria and her husband, Mannie, were people that his mama and dad used to spend time with as couples. So, without Duarte, it is much harder. Without money, it is harder still.

Maria is also collecting items from the foodbank.

He often feels ashamed to be here, but seeing Maria

reminds him that all families can fall on hard times. He waves hello across the room.

Maria smiles and moves straight over to where he is. 'Look at you, it's good to see you! How are you? The very image of your father, handsome boy. Growing up so fast. You must have grown a foot, at least.'

He beams. He loves being compared to his father.

'And how is your mama? I have not seen her for so long.'

He doesn't want to go there, so he asks Maria how she is as a way to dodge the question.

'Ah, well, I'm here because Mannie and I have both lost our jobs. The factory is going into receivership. These are hard times.'

He nods.

'But enough about me. How is your mama?' Maria is persistent. 'How is she doing? I must pop round to see her. It's been ages since we last got together.'

He shrugs. He doesn't want to lie, but he doesn't want to tell her the truth. He can't say the words.

Maria narrows her eyes and gives him a long, hard look. 'Tell you what, I will come home with you. I can give you a lift. It looks as if you have a lot of stuff to carry there.'

'I'm fine. I can manage,' he protests. Maria can't come into the house. She can't see his mama sitting on the sofa like a zombie staring out of the window at nothing. 'I have my brothers outside to help me. We won't all fit in.'

'Ah, those lovely boys. Even more reason that I should come with you. I'd like to say hello to them, too.'

There is no arguing with her.

'I have my car parked outside.' She smiles a rueful smile. 'Though for how much longer, I don't know. So we should make the most of it before I have to sell her.'

Maria helps him to finish gathering items, loading him up with plenty of food and household things. She carries her own groceries and some of his over to her little silver car.

'I'm keeping the car going with my savings while I try to get another job,' she explains. 'I've been applying for everything I can.'

Tomas doesn't remember Maria, but the other boys do and they squash in the back of the car while he sits up front with Maria. It's actually very nice to have a lift for once and not have to carry all the heavy stuff up the road.

As they approach their house, he undoes his seatbelt and runs round to open the door for his brothers and take the food from the back of the car. He is anxious to make a quick getaway, but as he stands at the back of the car, lowering the boot door, Maria is already out of the driver's seat and standing by the front door.

'I'd like to see your mama.'

He hangs his head. 'She's sleeping.'

Maria moves towards the lounge window. 'Hmm, I don't think so. I can see she is watching the TV. What are you trying to hide?'

'Oh.' He is running out of excuses. He should never have agreed to get into Maria's car.

'I want to see her. She's my friend – I miss her.'

She isn't going to take no for an answer.

He opens the door.

Maria walks straight into the lounge. 'Eliana?'

His mother will be furious. She wouldn't want Maria to see her like this. He shouldn't have accepted the lift. He doesn't want to bring shame on the family.

But it turns out to be one of the best things he's ever done.

Maria steps into their lives like some sort of Portuguese Mary Poppins. She visits every day after that, and brings another old friend, Beatrice, with her. Together, they force Eliana to get up from the sofa. The transformation is miraculous! Both in Eliana and in the house. First, they clean the place up. Properly. A real deep clean that it needs and hasn't had for a long time. They are methodical and go round room by room. They get rid of the empty bottles to the recycling centre and make no comment about it.

'You should have told me,' Maria says to Eliana. 'You should never have let things get like this.'

They make proper meals, batch-cooking so that there are extra portions in the fridge and the freezer to make it easy to heat up and cook when they aren't around. Beatrice works in a shop that sells Portuguese food and items.

It's a business that she set up with her husband and they are doing well because of the size of the local Portuguese community. It means they have a seemingly never-ending supply of the tinned sardine pate that is Eliana's favourite. But also lots of other, more traditional Portuguese meals, that cheer her and remind her of home.

He and his brothers have forgotten the taste of some of the dishes, but the flavours are so good that powerful memories from the past come rushing back with them.

Maria and Beatrice are a little dynamic duo. They make sure that beds are made, that uniforms are washed, that the house is aired, and that the cupboards are full. They bring fresh flowers which brighten the place up. They come in during the day when the boys are all at school, and when they get home, Eliana is up and about and busy, inspired by the intervention of her friends.

'I'm sorry,' Eliana says. 'I want to be better. I want to get better.'

Once order has been restored, it is friendship therapy. Maria and Beatrice force Eliana up and out of the house. They take her for drives out to places that are new, or they go for a walk. They also make her join a group for alcoholics.

Either Maria or Beatrice give Eliana some kind of nudge every day. They are determined that she will not drink. When they think she will be at her most vulnerable they call her, or pop over to see her. He has heard them say this is to break his mama's addiction circuit.

It means that, when the boys come home, they find their mama washed and dressed and, most important of all, smiling. Sometimes humming. It is as if their mama went away somewhere, at the same time as their dad, even though she barely left the house, and now she has come back. They all feel it.

It is wonderful to come in after school and find the house more like a home. The hours after school are no longer a time to be dreaded.

Today, Eliana is in the kitchen, which is spotless. She has prepared a picnic and packed a large bag with a football and other games that she has dug out of the shed.

'Go and change out of your uniforms and put your football boots on. We're going to the field!'

The field she means is next to the park. It has a large, mowed area where kids play football. Although there isn't a proper pitch marked out, there are goalposts.

They play football for an hour in the evening sunshine. It's late September now, but still feels like summer. It is huge fun. It's like the times before, when Duarte was still here. Eliana cheers and laughs.

'Diogo Jota!' Eliana calls when her son scores a goal. Not only is Diogo Jota a Liverpool legend, he is a *Portuguese* hero, and he is delighted with the comparison.

It's also been a long time since he's seen his brothers look so happy.

'You look like your father,' Eliana says. 'You have the same athletic build as Duarte. You are strong and fast like him,' she says, when he collapses down onto the grass next to where she is sitting. 'You can manoeuvre the ball with the same skill as he did.'

'The same?'

'Maybe not the same.'

'Oh.' He is disappointed.

'Perhaps better than Duarte.'

His heart soars. 'Do you miss him?' He dares to ask the question he never would have done while she was drinking.

'Of course I do. And I still love him. Wherever he is.'

'In Portugal.'

'In Portugal,' she agrees. 'But he doesn't love me. The way he left. It still makes no sense.' She shakes her head. 'But you, my son. You make sense. I like watching you all. My little men.'

While they have been tiring themselves out playing football, Eliana has set out the picnic.

The blankets are laid out and covered in a feast of goodies. There are Tupperware containers filled with savoury snacks, fresh bread, cured meats, different cheeses and seasonal fruits. It makes him happy to see all the Tupperware.

When they were little, his mama used to play a game where she'd put all the containers and lids out on the kitchen table and he and Andre would match the lids to the containers. There would be a prize for the winner, though he remembers that they all managed to 'win', even Tomas, because that's what his mama was like.

They take their time over the food, and when they are finished, the boys lie rolling on the blankets, laughing and winding each other up in the good-natured way of brothers.

Eliana jumps up, scooping up one of the Tupperware containers on her way. 'Let's pick some of those blackberries and I'll make a pie.'

'Yes!' He is delighted. It's late for blackberries but they're lucky, the good weather has kept them growing and it's been so long since they've done this. He loves his mama's blackberry pie.

It's one of the dishes that she learnt to bake when she first came to England. They scramble up to outdo each other in finding the biggest and the juiciest blackberries.

Most of the best ones are too big a stretch for Tomas,

but lifting Tomas up is the secret weapon to finding the shiny black jewels that are out of reach.

'We'll never make a pie if you eat them all as you go!' Eliana laughs.

'Good patch over here!' Dinis calls, finding a cache hidden behind another plant.

He wishes he had long trousers on, rather than shorts, so he could better fight his way through the prickly brambles. They find so many that he has to go back for more Tupperware to collect them all.

They all have purple sticky fingers and faces by the time they have finished, and enough blackberries to make a pie, freeze some, and fill the fruit bowl.

'What a magical evening!' Eliana sighs.

They return to the discarded picnic things and all help to gather and pack up the remains. Eliana folds up the blankets.

'Can we have one more game of football, before it gets dark?' he begs.

'Yes, yes, yes!' The other boys chorus.

Eliana smiles and sits on the bench facing the football field. 'Why not!'

But when he glances back, he sees that his mama is wringing her hands. Maria has warned him about this. She has warned him that it will be very hard, that his mama will be fighting, with all her might, not to give in, not to have a drink.

'She will crave it all the time. She will be desperate for a drink. It has been her friend for a long time. A very bad friend, it's true, but she will miss it all of the time.' Maria explained.

In spite of all the happiness, he has a sense of foreboding. They aren't out of the darkness. There is still a long way to go.

VI

Everything has become easier with Beatrice and Maria around. Maria, especially, is an ever-present force in their lives. She is so kind and gives so much of her time. He doesn't know what would have happened to them all if she hadn't appeared at the foodbank when she did.

'But it can't be forever,' she warns. She is looking for work herself and keeps them updated about her progress. 'I've got an interview for a care home job.'

'Oh.' He pauses. 'Good luck,' he remembers to add.

'Your mama should think about applying for jobs, too. It's the next step,' she tells him. 'It will do her good to have more structure and routine.'

Maria is very encouraging, but Eliana is resistant. She protests that she isn't ready yet. She is too early in her alcohol recovery.

It doesn't matter. He is not despondent. Maria might not get the job. And even if she does, Beatrice will be there to help with his mother's recovery and keep the family on the right track.

They are still poor, but they are managing. He still has to call in to the foodbanks on his way home, but the ladies there do look out for them. Andre is old enough to walk home with the two younger boys. He prefers going on his own. It's easier to slip in and out. He feels more shame when his siblings are waiting with him. All four of them looking poor and desperate is a bad feeling. He has a routine now, visiting different foodbanks on different days of the week.

He is still late for school sometimes, after dropping his brothers off, but Maria has helped Eliana to sort out free school lunches for him and for Andre now he has moved up. It happens with the thumbprint, so no one needs to know they're having free meals. They can just go into the canteen with everyone else. He doesn't have to rely on Jamie's generosity now. School is so much easier when he isn't hungry all day and he keeps his head down, away from the bullies.

But Beatrice also warns that things may have to change. 'I might not be around so much,' she says one afternoon. 'I'm going to have to focus on my business for a while. We're going to expand to frozen foods.'

Maria tuts. 'Why frozen foods, Beatrice? Why not fresh, good, healthy things?'

'Frozen is still healthy,' Beatrice says. 'It makes good business sense. Lots of our customers from the Portuguese community work long hours which means that they have little time to shop and cook. Having frozen foods will be popular and help busy parents who don't get home until after three, or five, or later, depending on their shift.'

He doesn't want Maria or Beatrice to work more and leave them. But perhaps things are solid enough now that Eliana could cope if they weren't there every day. Perhaps Eliana could even start a small job at Beatrice's family shop.

Maybe he should ask Beatrice if there could be a little job for his mama. He doesn't want charity, and he doesn't want to go behind his mother's back. But it would be good. It would be, like Maria says, the next step.

And Eliana has other friends now, new friends from the group for recovering alcoholics. They are good people who are on her team. He has a number to call if he is worried that she is going to 'relapse'.

So when Maria and Beatrice are around less, he will still have support. He will be 'the man'. He won't allow things to slip and get like they did before.

As the season deepens into autumn, the warm weather and sunshine disappear, and the temperature starts to drop. Eliana complains of being cold at home all day. 'I am moving around as much as I can and keeping myself busy with housework and cooking.'

'We could put the heating on,' he suggests, but Eliana shakes her head. They both know that they can't afford it.

Maria proposes a 'winter clothes sort out' and encourages Eliana to join in. Together they go through the boys' drawers and wardrobes to see what is good enough to pass on to the younger brothers and what new items the older boys need.

It will soon be half term and the shoes that they got from the foodbank are still in good shape, but all the boys are growing fast. 'Like weeds,' Maria jokes.

'They are all tall, like their father. Long legs and gangly,' Eliana says.

'Not an ounce of fat on any of them,' Maria agrees, shaking her head.

'But their father was a beanpole too. A tall, dark and handsome beanpole,' Eliana says.

'A tall, dark and handsome beanpole who left you!' Maria covers her mouth after the words have left it. 'I'm so sorry, Eliana, I didn't mean it like that.'

Eliana sobs. 'I miss him. I miss him every day. I miss him holding my hand.'

Maria holds her. 'I know you do, I know you do.'

He wants to talk more about his dad. He wants to know as much as he can, remember as much as he can. He wishes it didn't make his mama so sad to remember him.

'Back to the job in hand,' Maria says. 'The clothes!'

Eliana makes a list, with Maria's help, of what each boy needs. 'The plan is that we work on the principle of three of everything. One on, one in the wash and one fresh in the drawer.'

It doesn't sound like enough.

'It's old fashioned,' he protests.

'It's sensible,' Maria says. 'It was good enough for my parents, and it stops waste, something that we see a lot here in Liverpool.'

'Just Liverpool?' he asks.

'Don't be cheeky,' Eliana says. 'Listen to Maria. I guess that it must be the same across the country.'

They bag up all of the clothes that don't fit into the formula of three of everything. One bag is for the charity shop and there is another one for the recycling centre.

He is confused. 'Have we got this the right way round?' The clothes for recycling look in better condition than the charity shop ones.

'That's right,' Maria says, as she loads both black bin bags into the back of her car. 'I'll be the one doing the recycling – or rather, *upcycling* and *freecycling*.'

Maria is clever at making things. She also has access, through her friendship network, to a market of swapping and freecycling.

The following day, Maria returns with new jumpers and hoodies for each of the boys. She seems to be able to conjure up all sorts of things – of which warm clothes are just one example.

'Now that we've got all that sorted, would you like a lift to the foodbank?'

He nods. He's grateful for the offer. Especially today. The weather is grey and chilly and he came straight home from school because he didn't want to be outside too long. It will be lovely to be transported door to door.

Maria finds a parking space right outside the foodbank. He thanks her, opens the passenger door and walks into the familiar building.

As he enters, the ladies who volunteer regularly recognise him and smile and wave. He doesn't even have a chance to look at the food before one of them calls him over.

'Got something to show you today. Come and have a look!' She is holding a bag that they have kept back especially for him. It is filled with new, unwanted and unopened toys.

He looks inside and smiles. His younger brothers will love all this. 'Thank you. I really appreciate it. It's so kind,' he says.

'And there's something for you as well,' another of the ladies says. 'Maria told us that you and your brothers are massive football fans. She said that you were devastated when your football hero died.'

The lady is holding a large frame, but the wrong way round, so that he can only see the back of it.

The other women gather around expectantly. He frowns. He doesn't really know what's going on. The lady slowly turns it around so that he can see what's in the frame.

He gasps and brings both hands up to his mouth and chin. He isn't sure if it's for him or they are just showing it to him: a framed poster of Diogo Jota, almost life-sized.

'Someone brought it in as a donation,' the lady explains.

Maria is behind him. She puts her hand on his arm. 'It's for you,' she nods. 'I spotted it when I popped in earlier and I asked the ladies to save it for you,' she says.

'We hoped it might bring a little bit of joy to one of our favourite young people,' the lady holding the picture tells him. 'Do you like it?'

He nods and blushes, and suddenly feels himself welling up. He doesn't want to cry, but he can't help himself when people are so thoughtful.

'I don't know what to say. I can't believe it.'

The volunteers clap, as though it is his birthday.

He shakes his head gently, smiling. 'No, no. I can't believe it.'

'Well, you should believe it. Look.' Maria points at the words that are part of the image. He reads them out.

'The first step to achieve something is to believe.'

He is so pleased, so grateful.

He holds the frame in front of him, both arms outstretched, balancing it on the table so he can admire it.

'Honestly, I don't know what to say.'

'You don't have to say anything. That smile is enough,' the volunteer lady says. 'There's nothing more rewarding than helping someone smile.'

'Thank you.'

Maria helps to sort out the food with him, which is a good job because he is so moved that he can't think properly about what they need.

They gather all the basics and a few other bits. There is even a treat for his mama. 'Do you think she'd like this lovely box of Milk Tray?'

He knows she will. Eliana loves chocolate.

The volunteer squeezes his arm. 'We're always here for you. You know that. Come back soon.'

He is still on cloud nine when he steps back outside.

He waits outside with the bags and his picture, while Maria goes to get her car. A black Ford Fiesta with two young men in the front is parked across the road, but he doesn't really register it, because he is still thinking about the picture and the very kind ladies in the food bank.

Sometimes, when he is being bullied at school, or he thinks about the way his father was treated, he concludes that people are mean.

The world is just filled with bad people. Today, he

thinks that the world is a place filled with good people, who do nice things.

When Maria pulls up onto the pavement, he catches sight of the two men in the black Ford Fiesta looking over at him. Perhaps they are waiting to go to the foodbank, although they don't look the sort. Perhaps they are admiring his new picture.

He puts the food on the back seats with the bag of toys for his brothers. He sits in the passenger seat, holding the frame, staring down at the picture. He plans to take an old picture down from the wall in his room that he shares with Andre. He'll put this up in its place, so he can see it when he is in bed.

'I love this, Maria,' he says. 'Thank you.'

'No need. You deserve it. I know how hard you work for your brothers and your mama.'

When they reach home, Maria stays seated in her car.

'Can you manage the bags and the picture, alright? I won't come in today. I need to get back. I got the job in the care home.'

'Congratulations!' he says, automatically. Selfishly, he wishes she hadn't got the job. Maria has become like a second mama these last few months. And without Beatrice, too, how will Eliana cope? How will they all cope? He knows he's going to have to step up again.

'That's really good news.'

'It is. And I really need it. But you know what it means–?'

'We won't be seeing so much of you.'

'That's right. The hours I'll be working at the care home means that I won't be able to help out as much here as I have been.' She puts her hand on his arm. 'But you don't need me anymore,' she adds, quickly. 'Your mama is so much better. You've got everything under control. With you by her side–'

'We'll be fine,' he says bravely. 'Don't worry about us. You need to earn your money. You have bills to pay. We'll be just fine.'

He isn't sure that's true. He'll have to get back on top of the household budgeting. They have about £300 per week for all five of them. It sounds like a lot, but it has to cover everything.

'Good luck!'

Maria waves goodbye, smiles and drives away.

A black car, that looks just like the one he saw at the foodbank drives past too.

I

PART TWO

Louise

Today I'm felling a tree in the garden. Well, not by myself. It's a two-person job. My husband, Lloyd, is helping me, and loving his lumberjack impersonation. The tree is a cross between a pear and apple tree and has produced tons of fruit – all of which tasted absolutely disgusting.

I originally planted it near the wall that separates us from our neighbours, partly to create a green screen in that part of the garden and partly to cover up the wall. I don't like bare brick walls.

For the first year, all was good. The tree grew well and had a nice, straight trunk. Then it began to lean. We propped it up and gave it some support, but it became so heavy with the vile pear-apples that it leaned almost right over to the end wall, and it just looks wrong. Coupled with the inedible fruit, we've decided it can't stay.

The other tree in this bit of the garden is the apple tree that Dotty is buried beneath. Dotty, our beloved family pet of nearly 14 years, who died in the spring. I must say, the apples are beautiful this year. So, thank you, Dotty.

It's been a weird summer in terms of weather. We managed to eat outside plenty of times in June and July but, as usual, the sunny, warm weather disappeared the moment the children broke up for school holidays. It's as if the weather likes to laugh at us.

The kids tend to stay inside when the weather is rubbish, unless we pay a small fortune to take them out. This weekend we have decided to do some jobs that have needed doing for a while. 'No more excuses' is the mantra.

Lloyd loves his chainsaw. If there is an opportunity to use it, he will. With extra loud revs for good measure. Now that the tree is down, he's cutting up the felled branches into logs that we will store away to dry out and season. I'm doing the stacking and storing. The pattern is the same as when we're in the kitchen.

He loves cooking, and I love him to cook. But I end up clearing it all up afterwards. Unsurprisingly, I am bent over, breaking twigs and sticks to fit into a large green garden bag that, for some reason I can't fathom, smells of toilets.

It isn't often we do jobs together, we aren't that sort of couple. Probably because we have different views about how they should be carried out. Sometimes I end up mumbling under my breath.

'Did you say something?' Lloyd will ask.

When called out in this way, I always make out I was talking to Doug, my remaining pooch, another jackhuahua. Since Dotty died, Douglas has howled in the garden every morning. It's quite plaintive, as if he's saying, 'Dot, why have you left me on my own with this lot?'

The other thing we've noticed, now that he is a widower, is that he has become fat. I think it's because we all keep spoiling him. These days he has a tin of tuna, or slices of roast chicken, or some freshly-grilled sausages. Gone are the days of kibble and dog food. Soon he'll have a seat at the table with his own plate, starters, main and pudding.

I think I need to walk him more.

The last evidence of the tree's existence is raked away and the afternoon is gone. The weekend is over too soon.

I love these late summer weekends. When the day ends, Lloyd makes a cocktail. We have a tea towel framed on the wall in the kitchen that has all the classic cocktail recipes on it. Each cocktail has a lovely illustration to go with it. It's a work of art. Once upon a time I wouldn't have put something like that on the wall, but the social workers have loosened up on their anti-any-fun attitudes to foster carers in the last couple of years. They always used to – and some sometimes still do – warn us to 'hide all your alcohol away'. I've never agreed with the approach. I think it's daft. In my view, seeing adults drink sensibly must be better than pretending alcohol doesn't exist. In my childhood home, alcohol was considered to be the devil's work, so nothing was ever drunk, only stored away in the MFI sideboard cabinet in the dining room.

Consequently, I wasted no time in mastering the art of knocking back the unwanted Christmas presents of cherry brandy, sloe gin, or even advocaat, long before I reached the legal drinking age – ensuring that I topped the bottle up with water from the downstairs cloakroom to disguise the illicit consumption,.

Moreover, my adoptive family's disgust at the act of drinking, and condemnation of all those who did, later pushed me firmly through the doors of nearly all of the pubs in Oxford.

So, with the voice of experience, I say a very loud 'no' to locking the alcohol away and 'yes' to just being sensible with it. So many foster carers are leaving the system that I'm sure social workers have had to become more realistic with their expectations. Foster carers come from all backgrounds and experiences. They each have their own lives to lead and sometimes a glass of wine is the only way to end a tough day with the foster children.

Because, let's be honest about this, foster children

themselves are nothing like what foster children used to be when they invented the rules of this weird world of fostering. Children who come into care these days are usually the children who have had unlimited and unsupervised access to smart phones since they were toddlers. They have been exposed to porn, predators, marketing, fake news and many idiotic views of the world. In the context of dealing with all of that, a glass of wine seems quite tame. The old world view of fostering doesn't fit with today's young people at all. Anyway, I digress. It must be the cocktail.

It's Sunday evening. I take a long, luxurious bath after my exertions with the leaning tree of doom-fruit, and enjoy the feeling of being clean in my gorgeous cotton pyjamas. I'm getting ready for an evening of film and, hopefully, no bother from the children, Jackson and Vincent, my birth sons, and our long-term foster daughter Lily. The boys are gaming with each other from the splendid isolation of their own rooms. The language from Vincent is a little on the 'colourful' side and I have to call out, 'Vincent!' several times.

Each occasion elicits a 'sorry, Mum', but then, 10 minutes later, he forgets himself and is back swearing and sounding like he's in a street fight. It amazes me the way he can sound so foul and dreadful, then trip lightly downstairs and say, 'Hi, Mum, have you had a nice afternoon?' in a sing-song voice – as though there are two Vincents with entirely different vocabularies inside the one body.

The latter usually has an ulterior motive, though: he will be on the hunt for edible goodies. Arms and pockets loaded with snacks, he'll troop back upstairs to shout and swear loudly at more people. You have to love technology. Who would have thought this would become our normal?

The following morning, I wake up early and make coffee. While the coffee machine is doing its thing, I put a load of washing on. Next, I go to stack some more things in the dishwasher. I open the dishwasher door to discover that not only has it not been emptied, but new, dirty bowls have been put in the top along with the clean dishes.

Oh, joy.

Food gunk has dripped down and made the clean stuff dirty again. One of those extra little irritations that could so easily have been avoided. It's all I can do to prevent myself from growling. Got to love 'labour-saving' devices in the hands of teenagers. At least the cutlery basket seems okay. I pull the knives out and put them in their place in the big drawer, followed by the forks, then the spoons.

I have a memory of being at a boyfriend's parents' house when I was about the age of 14. His family were the first people I knew who had a dishwasher. My boyfriend's dad was an architect. I remember him placing the cutlery in the kitchen drawer so carefully. Not like me. I sort of throw them in and they land where they land; he placed all the forks on top of each other and end to end, so that they lined up perfectly, nestled together. The spoons, too. After they'd been in the dishwasher and before he put them away, he wiped them with a tea towel. I don't do that either. I literally grab them from the cutlery tray and sling them in the drawer – then avoid looking too deeply at the smears. Did people have more time in the 80s?

I take my coffee and sit sipping it on the garden bench facing down the garden. A little morning reflection time. We have had a couple of different children here for the summer holidays, on 'respite'. Some people hate that term, preferring 'sleepovers' as a way of describing the short-term breaks for foster carers to allow them a much-needed rest and recharge while supporting a child in care. I'm not sure the children themselves care what it's called. But then, they don't do the paperwork.

We did three weeks in total over the summer. One boy for one week and then two little girls together for two weeks. It meant that their foster carers could go on holiday, have a break and some time to themselves, and also avoid the expense of having to pay for multiple mouths while they're away, so perhaps eating out more than they would if they were at home. I'm aware that some people think it's terrible for foster carers to leave their foster children while they take a break. To them, I say, 'You try to look after these smartphone junkies and see how you get on without a break.'

The little boy we looked after in the first week was delightful. He was so easy-going, it was no trouble. The sisters, on the other hand, who we had for a fortnight, were hard work. They had been with their carers for two years. The foster carers had evidently done a lot of work with them, but you could see that the dynamic between the girls was challenging. The youngest one was a thug; she enjoyed hurting her big sister, who was very patient with whatever came her way, until she was pushed too far. It's fair to say we were quite glad to wave goodbye to those two at the end of their stay. I was exhausted by the constant bickering and moaning. When we're acting as respite carers, we don't invest too much emotionally. I think, for the children, it can feel a little bit like staying with your favourite uncle and aunty who let you stay up late and eat sweets. We tend to let the boundaries and rules slip in a way that we don't for longer-term foster children, framing their stay as a holiday.

After coffee, I shower, get dressed and decide that I will hit the ground running! But instead I have another coffee, realise that I haven't fully recovered from the last 'holiday' and wonder why I do this to myself.

The phone goes before I reach the bottom of the second cup.

It's Kendi, our supervising social worker. He has been with us for a couple of years now, which is a bit of a coup in itself. When I talk to fellow foster carers, I discover that some are still waiting for any supervising social worker at all. We're lucky to have the consistency. Not only has Kendi been with us for a good length of time, he is wonderful. I love his laidback manner – that isn't really laidback at all when you see how much he manages to get done. I think being a supervising social worker might be a tad easier than being a children's social worker, which, if I'm honest, looks like a hell of a job.

It's easy to see why so many are leaving the sector when you factor in all the cutbacks. Less money leads to the availability of fewer and fewer resources, and ultimately makes the job far, far more difficult than it should be. Many end up working above and beyond their hours, putting their hands in their own pockets at times to cover shortfalls, out of their own kindness. It's the usual situation: the system relies on the good nature of its employees to deliver. Because they do so, it excuses the authorities from having to do it. *It makes me so cross.*

'Can you have a look at the email I've sent, Louise?' Kendi asks.

'On my way.' I head over to my studio with the remainder of my second coffee in hand. Lloyd is still snoozing in bed. I can be sure of this because I hear him snoring from downstairs. Every time I mention his snoring he claims he doesn't snore. How he can be so adamant given that he's asleep when it happens is a mystery. I think I may have to record him so he understands the extent of the issue.

I lift the laptop lid, sit down and click onto the referral that has come through, for a boy called 'Diego Martins'.

I skim read the details. This first thing that strikes me is that there is no mention of where he's from. That can mean out of county. The first warning sign.

'So, what's this about, then, Kendi?' I ask.

'It looks like the boy has got into some trouble,' Kendi starts to say.

'Now, you know that's not what happened. The trouble has found the child. That's how this goes.'

'Carry on reading,' Kendi urges.

I skim the referral. 'Where is he from? There's no current location on this.'

'Deliberately,' Kendi says. 'For the last few months he's been in different cities around the UK. Leeds. Liverpool. Lancaster.'

'Only places beginning with L? In the north? Right. Okay, so tell me what's really going on here.'

There is a short pause on the other end of the line, then Kendi makes a 'hmmm' sound.

I shake my head, though Kendi can't see it. 'Kendi,

are we looking at a young man who is on the run from county lines?'

There are a few clues – not least the removal of this child from his home county to the other end of the country. I used to think that the phrase 'county lines' had overtones of the Wild West and sheriffs with no jurisdiction beyond their county boundaries.

In reality, I'm all too familiar with it these days as a term used to describe gangs and organised criminal networks that are involved in moving illegal drugs around the country using dedicated mobile phone lines or other forms of 'deal line'. Gangs exploit children and vulnerable adults, so they can move and store the drugs and money, and use coercion, intimidation and violence to make it happen.

'Now, hold your horses. We don't know that for sure, Louise.'

'Kendi, I wasn't born yesterday.'

He chuckles.

There are also references to a stabbing, and mention of sexual exploitation.

'Anything else you can tell me that might help us make a decision?'

'Not specifically, but I know that, whatever happens, you'll make the right decision.'

I *hate* it when he says things like that!

When Lloyd comes downstairs a little while later, I make him a coffee.

'So, brace yourself. We've received a referral that Kendi's keen for us to consider.'

He's still yawning when I hand him the printout. 'He sounds like a smart kid. He's Portuguese and has a big family.'

'Portuguese?'

Lloyd and I went to Portugal when I was pregnant with Jackson and we loved it. The Atlantic sea was cold. That's about the only thing that wasn't perfect about Portugal, as far as I can remember.

'Yes. The family has been living in Liverpool.'

Lloyd looks at me, sighs, and says, 'Ah. So, if they're sending him all the way down here, then county lines?'

'Kendi isn't naming county lines, of course.'

'Well, he wouldn't, would he?' Lloyd says.

No one likes to, and that's partly why it has been allowed to become so big and unstoppable. In other countries cartels are talked about, but in England we simply don't know what to say.

We decide to consider it. Children involved in county lines are children. Fact. They have been exploited and used, and whatever has happened will, no doubt, not have been their fault. But that doesn't stop us from feeling scared by the idea of having one stay with us.

I spend a disturbing few hours Googling 'county lines'. First hit is the National Crime Agency. There is a picture of a teenager and, where his eyes should be, the word 'victim' is written. *Dan, 16, has been stabbed and forced to sell drugs miles away from home.*

Next is the Met Police. Their website refers to OCGs, or organised crime groups. I have to refamiliarise myself with the acronym, although we've had several brushes with children connected to county lines in the last few years, and I've encountered girls who've been caught up in county lines through my work with the charity Spark Sisterhood.

The last one I look at is the Children's Society. A cute, freckled boy stares out at me. *Children as young as seven are targeted*, the website warns. Diego has only just turned 14.

I call Kendi and ask a few more questions.

'And I need to know the answers, Kendi. This is all to do with safety. Our safety.'

Kendi has been busy speaking to the team who've been looking after Diego and can fill in some of the gaps in the referral.

Diego has been removed from his home town where he was recruited as a 'soldier' and mule for Bulgarian and Albanian gangs. He has been stabbed and sexually exploited by the gang's leader.

'But what you must know, Louise, is that before that,

Diego was a loyal, hard-working student who looked after his family because his mother had become an alcoholic.'

My heart is already going out to him.

Kendi also tells me that Diego has not seen his family for four months, and has been moved to multiple different locations as he was wanted by the gang – who had tried to kill him before he was removed. He witnessed a murder, which is why he has been put into protection.

'He'll need lots of nurture and support to help him with his post-traumatic stress,' Kendi explains.

Ain't that the truth.

I can't make a decision yet. I wait all day to see how I feel. Thoughts circle around my head: what if he was my son? What if it was Jackson or Vincent who'd been coerced into county lines and witnessed a murder? I feel stressed just thinking about it.

I go back to Lloyd, talking to him in between his online meetings. I explain all the details that Kendi has teased out of the team in the north. They are a private organisation. I suspect the local authority would not have the expertise or resources to deal with something like this.

At dinner, I watch the boys and Lily as they go about their business, thinking about their safety. As a parent, or a carer, you never switch off from thinking about safety. You're always making sure that the environment is safe: looking out for hazards. Sharp edges, electric sockets, breakable ornaments when they're very little. I've never wanted to wrap them up in cotton wool, but I want to know if, by inviting Diego into our home, we would somehow be putting them in direct danger. The very opposite of what a parent or carer is supposed to do. What if this boy tried to recruit or exploit them? What if they got caught up in his world?

Then I remember Diego's age. He is younger than both of my sons. He is a child. He has been caught up in something created by adults. He isn't the problem.

After dinner, I'm clearing up while Lloyd sits at the table announcing that he's tired. I do manage to bite my lip at that, but my plate-stacking might be a fraction louder and my wiping down of the kitchen counter a tad more aggressive than normal – momentarily.

I raise the subject of Diego once more.

'At least we know what's going on with him, I suppose,' Lloyd says.

Not all of it, of course, how can we ever know someone else's life completely? But Lloyd's right. So often, when new children come into our home, we have very little idea of what's been happening in their lives. For once, we have a very clear picture. It isn't a pretty one, but at least we know what it is. I'm drawn to him precisely because I know that he will be difficult to find a placement for – with good reason. Under these exceptional circumstances, there won't be many families keen to take him.

'What does your gut say?' I ask him.

'My gut says he's probably fine and, if he's not, the company that has responsibility for him will take him away again.'

He isn't coming via the usual route of local authority or an independent fostering agency that we know. Instead, there is a company, or possibly a charity, or CIC (community interest company), I'm not sure. They're called 'Freeedom', which I thought was a spelling mistake when I first saw it.

With that reassurance in the background we decide that, if the kids are up for it, we'll go for it. I visit each of the children in their rooms with the proposal. I don't tell them the details. Instead, I keep it very simple.

'How do you feel about a young boy – he's 14 – called Diego coming to stay for a bit? He's Portuguese and from somewhere up north. He's had a bit of a tough time.'

They are all experienced foster siblings.

They all say yes.

11

Diego is coming in four days' time, this Friday. The speed at which things have moved is somewhat frightening. I wake up in the night wondering if we have done the wrong thing. I keep calling Kendi to check on things as they occur to me. It's all about wanting to know if we will be safe with Diego in the house. If the children will be safe. Of course, he says the right things, but he can only assure me so far: up to the line of 'insurance' and 'policy'.

I think, these days, they have become the same thing. He is one sentence away from giving me gentle platitudes – which is un-Kendi-like and might signal the end of our successful working relationship. The moment a social worker dishes out meaningless platitudes, I can't take them seriously anymore.

Kendi gives me the number for Simon, the social worker who works for Freeedom. It goes to voicemail and the recorded message explains that he is one of Freeedom's 'relocation managers'. That they need more than one 'relocation manager' is perhaps an indication of the scale of the county lines problem. I leave a message and resist the urge to ask if Simon spells his name with additional vowels.

Simon calls me back in the afternoon. I'm momentarily surprised when the call comes through via WhatsApp. Simon has a warm voice as he introduces himself. He is friendly and reassuring and explains that it is safer to talk on WhatsApp because the platform is protected by encryption. He will speak and send all messages via WhatsApp; there will be no emails that reference Diego. He thanks me for being willing to welcome Diego and tells me a bit about his own background.

'I started my career in the police, then retrained to be a social worker, and then began volunteering to help kids get away from crime in Glasgow.'

He is also now one of the directors of Freeedom. 'But I prefer to be at the coalface rather than in the office. I like working with young people. I don't want to be stuck behind a desk.'

He tells me more about the work that Freeedom does. They have a team of ex-gang members in the company: men and women who have managed to get away from criminal involvement themselves, and want to support children and youths to escape too. They come from all over the country and they tend not to work in the areas where they worked for gangs. Many of them became involved in county lines as children and were criminalised as a result.

'Part of what we do, as well as relocating children like Diego, is about shifting attitudes. It's starting to happen – slowly,' he explains. 'Instead of criminalising them, now there's a greater movement towards seeing children and young people as victims of exploitation.'

This is all music to my ears. I have listened to the police on the news and at local and regional events over the years, where they talk about children and their families in such derogatory ways that it makes me want to *scream*.

But I also know that it's not just the child who becomes involved with the exploitation; it can be the whole family who get dragged in. Just thinking about it makes me worried. I am conjuring up the worst scenarios in my head. I see carloads of men in hoodies with knives and guns outside our house. My children being threatened, my pets slaughtered.

I explain some of my concerns to Simon.

He is kind and completely understands. 'So, Diego has been moved four times already to ensure safety. This has happened by swapping cars and travelling in the night. We run a professionally-organised operation and hide young people like Diego until we believe it's safe.'

'So, Kendi, our supervising social worker who you've been liaising with, tells me that Diego witnessed a murder?'

'He did. He then managed to flee the scene and went missing for a few weeks. No one knew where he was or if he was okay. Then he showed up at a police station where he tried to hand himself in, but he hadn't committed a crime; he'd seen one. He was put into witness protection initially, then he was moved to us at Freeedom because he's a minor. But the team he was assigned to didn't have capacity to work with a minor at that time. Witness protection is never straightforward, but in Diego's case he also needed care. He couldn't just be moved to a safehouse. So, for the last four months, he's stayed in various different safe locations, and has also had to adapt the way he looks several times.'

It's quite a story. 'That's an awful lot for a kid to go through,' I say.

'Yes. A lot for anyone to go through. But he's a good kid.'

'And what kind of support is he receiving for the post-traumatic stress that I assume he's suffering?' I ask.

Simon is candid and I like it. 'Because of the nature of the crime and what we know about those who committed it, he can't receive standard mental health support. We can't use his name because, believe it or not, these facilities sometimes have contacts within them from the gangs. They literally have tentacles everywhere, so we run a very tight and secure operation. His birth name is not Diego

Martins. But it's the name we're working with for now. He chose his first name, Diego, after his favourite sporting legend.'

My knowledge of most sports isn't great, to be fair; I won't be winning *Mastermind* with anything connected to sport as the specialist subject, but I do recognise the name of a legend.

'Is that Diego Maradona?'

Simon laughs. 'Not Maradona. Though you're right, he *is* also a Diego. No, our boy has named himself after Diogo Jota.'

Who I think I have also heard of, but I'm not sure why.

'He's a Portuguese footballer,' Simon says, probably sensing my confusion. 'Or, I should say, he was. And Diego's the Spanish version of Diogo, to hide the Portuguese connection with his birth family. We only refer to him as 'Diego' and we can't share with you his birth name. Diego has been told not to give or use his birth names – ever.'

It all sounds very cloak and dagger, and I have the slightly sick feeling of wondering whether I'm doing the right thing again. It would be very easy to just walk away from this now. Part of me wants to. The other part of me is excited to help.

'Now, when we arrive on Friday, Louise, will your husband be at home? We need to give you both a full briefing and ensure that you and your family are aware of all the protocols and make sure that you feel safe.'

Simon's tone is warm, but all of a sudden, I don't feel safe.

'We are only one call away at all times of the day and night and can get an agent to you within an hour, but would always recommend that you call 999 if you have any concerns of immediate threat.'

Immediate threat? What the hell are we doing?

'Your address will be flagged from Friday on the system as a 'safe house' but no more information will be given. If you do have to call 999, the police will know to call our team and, as I say, we're available 24/7.'

'Look, I'm not so sure now. I haven't explained too much to the children, and I don't know–'

'Probably the right move,' Simon says. 'And all to the good. You don't want to scare or excite them. Experience has shown that it's best to offer a light touch awareness to children. They can accidentally let things slip and information can travel fast in a world of smartphones.'

'Yes, it can.'

Simon manages to reassure me that they will protect Diego and my family.

When I get off the phone, I feel a weird mixture of fear and excitement.

Being a foster carer can certainly lead you in some

interesting directions, and being part of an operation to protect a young person from criminal gangs feels rather exciting.

This is a big deal.

It's also exacerbated by my own ex-care-system-kid adrenaline.

Worried by how he's going to take it, I convey everything that Simon said to Lloyd. I can see his face light up; he loves the whole idea straight away. Lloyd is a funny blend of ex-punk/indie rebellion and sensible middle-age. He used to look like Robert Smith from The Cure but, with his parents' naval background he is also deeply patriotic. Not in that naff, untrue, parasitical way that the right wing uses, but totally respectful of all our defence services and grateful to all those who lost their lives to keep us all safe. He is totally onboard and can't wait for the briefing. He never fails to amaze me.

Kendi calls. 'How are you?'

I have calmed down, now that I feel that Lloyd is going to turn our home into Bletchley Park and will probably have tea-stained paper maps all over the kitchen walls. Metaphorically, at least. The cocktail tea towel is probably safe for now. Lloyd will have everything set up on his computer and phone.

Oh no! The phone!

I am the tech-luddite of the house. I hope there aren't

going to be any great expectations that I can do techie things... I'll worry about that next.

'I'm fine,' I tell him. And for the first time in a few days, it's true. My mind turns to practical matters. 'I'm guessing that Diego won't have much stuff with him.'

'Very likely,' he agrees. 'Perhaps a bag of clothes. Not much more. The boy is not allowed any tech, of course, in case the gang find him online and attempt to communicate with him via his gaming devices, for example. He is certainly not allowed to have a phone, but he knows this and accepts it. And Freeedom will be checking in regularly to see if he is okay, as well as you and the rest of your family, Louise.'

I ask if we are expecting a decent allowance in exchange for this witness protection work.

Kendi is surprised by my request.

'To be fair, Kendi, this is not normal fostering, is it?'

There is danger and extra vigilance and involvement of additional services. A lot is being asked of us that does not normally happen, 'So, I want to know what our allowance is.'

'Well, I haven't done anything about that.'

I don't know what's going on with Kendi lately. He used to be much more on the foster carers' side, and overtly savvy. To have understood all the additional implications in this case and not to have asked for an uplift is a bit remiss of him.

'I feel very strongly about this, Kendi,' I persist. 'Diego is not a normal fostering placement. This is witness protection and it's my family and home that's providing the venue and cover for that.'

'I'll speak to my manager.'

This is not like Kendi at all. He has turned into a compliant poodle where he used to be a bulldog. The reason that his team of foster carers like him so much is because we trust him to advocate for the carers and the children, not to spout management-speak. I let it go for now, but I must admit, I am rather disgruntled about this side of things.

I talk to Lloyd about Kendi, sharing my concerns that one of the best social workers we have ever met is becoming like all the others.

'I wouldn't read too much into it, Louise,' Lloyd says. He's probably under the cosh of his manager. You know how it is. They're all under pressure not to spend money.'

But saving money is the very last thing that should be happening right now for children in care who already have so little.

'Whatever. I'm still finding it annoying that Kendi is being pathetic. We need social workers with backbone or nothing gets done.'

Soon the boys – and later Lily – are home. As they plunder the fridge and raid all the cupboards, I feel like

I'm being burgled. They ping about the kitchen, dropping bags onto the floor. Jackson puts his down on the table, a thing that drives me mad. I remove it and drop it with the others onto the floor, reminding them that their bags have been on grubby floors. 'And we *eat* at the table!'

They pay no attention; they are on a mission to eat. I say, 'Diego is arriving on Friday during the day. He'll be here by the time you get home from school. Can you please be nice to him? He's travelling from Wales, so he'll have had a long journey.' Apparently that's hideout number four, but I omit to tell them that bit.

Knowing that Diego will be with us soon, I begin to prepare the house. I look around his room and decide to buy some new bedding in town. The poor boy has been through a lot. He named himself after a sports person. It was a name close to 'Diego'. I Google 'Diogo, sport' and find several footballers. I wonder if he likes football. I remember Simon said that one of the places he lived was Liverpool, so I try 'Diogo Footballer Liverpool' and find Diogo Jota. I read his story, that he died in a car accident with his brother. It sounds tragic.

I message Simon. *Does Diego support Liverpool?*

Within seconds, I receive a message back. *Yes, a big Liverpool fan.*

I've got three days left to do this room. I scrap the bedding from town idea and go online to find Liverpool bedding. I also find a poster of Diogo Jota. I check the size and realise I've got frames to put it in. The asking about the allowance goes out of the window. I know, as a seasoned foster carer, that this is the most important bit – and I always end up funding it myself. Making a child feel welcome, valued and thought of is something that the teeny-weeny fostering allowances do not recognise.

The rest is left blank until he gets here. He needs to be able to put his own stamp on the place.

Meanwhile, I concentrate on my husband's weird excitement and, to be fair, my own, to be working with Diego and Freeedom.

III

Friday comes and Lloyd is more excited than he usually is about the arrival of a new placement to our house. He is all over this! The door goes and he almost pushes me out of the way in his eagerness to get there. I'm amused by this: perhaps I can somehow exploit it, so that this time round Lloyd takes the lion's share of work. We'll see…

There are four people standing behind the glass in the front door. As Lloyd opens it, it strikes me that another world waits outside on the step. Lloyd reaches out and shakes all their hands.

I am overwhelmed by the scale of the operation. Three adults for one little boy.

Simon walks in first and strides towards me to shake my hand. He has a touch of the hippy about him, mixed in with someone who earns some decent cash. He is wearing a Rolex.

The other two adults are introduced as Ross and Ben. They look to be in their late 20s, maybe early 30s, and are dressed in hoodies and jeans. I know Simon has warned me that many of Freeedom's workers are ex-gang members, but these look like current gangsters, if I'm honest.

Diego stands between them, but hangs back slightly. I notice a huge black 4x4 with shiny wheels parked outside. The neighbours will be twitching,

I already feel like I'm in a movie.

I concentrate on the star of it: the young boy standing between the very tall and gym-tastic Ross and Ben.

'Hi, Diego, I'm Louise. Come on in.'

Our kitchen is big. Bigger than most kitchens, I'd say, but with four tall, broad men in it, plus Diego and me, it feels tiny.

Poor Doug goes and lies down on his bed, unamused by the way his house is being taken over by humans who aren't that interested in him.

It all feels a bit awkward, so I ask if anyone wants a drink. They all do.

Diego asks for a cold drink. 'Sitting in the car listening to Ross's crap music all the way has made me thirsty.'

It's a good way to break the ice, because Ross and Ben laugh and call Diego a philistine.

It's a bit of a cheeky first remark, but I like that he has character. Ross and Ben want cold drinks too. I offer diet cokes, as we only have diet fizzy drinks in our house, and I wouldn't even have those if I had my own way. Simon eyes up our coffee machine and asks for a black coffee, the same as Lloyd. It takes a little while to provide all the drinks. It feels like a lot of people and I can only make one coffee at a time. I give up and don't bother with one for myself.

I supply plenty of Fox's biscuits and cookies which go down rather well. Simon looks around the kitchen appraisingly. 'I think you've landed on your feet, here, Diego.'

Diego nods enthusiastically. 'Yeah, thanks, Simon. Louise, you have a really nice home.' He's more confident than I expected and seems mature for 14. Obviously having spent time in the company of older men, he has all the banter. Though we are not allowed to have 'banter' officially, as it can be offensive, but you know what I mean. Gawd, it's hard talking and writing these days.

Simon makes himself the chair of the meeting, and we're just settling to it when the door goes. I get up to open it. It's Kendi. I had almost forgotten him. I'm friendly, but not as much as I usually am. I'm not 'feeling the love' right now. Kendi's arrival adds to the Tall Man group and, not only am I feeling very outnumbered, but the kitchen feels like a doll's house.

Simon gets up to shake hands with Kendi. They have spoken a few times on the phone so are already acquainted, but there are further introductions to Ross and Ben, and to Diego.

I sit down again and Simon starts the conversation with a big thank you to Lloyd and me. Then he outlines the reason why these 'unusual circumstances' prevail today.

In front of Diego he says, 'Diego is a good lad, but he, like so many young people, got caught up in county lines activity because he was vulnerable.'

Ross and Ben nod in agreement.

As Simon goes on to tell us about the reasons why all this has happened and the fact that Diego has witnessed a murder, I notice that Diego lowers his eyes and begins staring intently at his own hands.

'It was a horrific crime and Diego is still suffering from PTSD,' Simon says.

I knew this was a huge undertaking, but suddenly the full intensity and reality of the situation begins to hit. This is not an exciting adventure. Not for Diego, and it shouldn't be for us. I watch Diego's hands; his fingers are very busy. I have seen this before. When Simon pauses, I ask Diego what support he has been receiving.

He looks at Simon and then says, 'This bunch of weirdos.'

Everyone smiles. I like Diego already. He is good humoured, in spite of all that's happened to him and, unsurprisingly, old before his time.

After some banal paperwork, Ben asks Diego if he wants to go for a drive around the area.

'That's a good idea,' I agree. 'Will Diego be going to our local school? You could head in that direction.'

Simon says, 'Yes, that's the plan and it's all arranged.'

I like this level of organisation. Many times in the past, when a child has arrived with us, I've had to do plenty of the organisational legwork.

'He's a clever lad,' Simon continues, 'and needs to get back on his game.'

I explain the directions for the school. Ben asks if Diego can see his room before they head off.

'Of course, follow me,' I say. As I leave the kitchen to walk up the stairs, Doug gets off his bed to follow.

'Wow, your house is cool,' Diego says as we pass through the hall. Ben agrees.

I thank them and smile inside, knowing full well what a difference art and paintings can make to any environment.

We reach the door to his room and I open it, so that he and Ben can walk in. Diego smiles as he sees all the Liverpool-themed bedding and shares a look with Ben.

'You're a thoughtful lady, Louise. This is really kind. Diego's going to feel very at home here. That was a nice thing to do.'

I'm pleased, because after swathing the bed in red, I had wondered if it might be too childish for a teenager.

Diego looks at the framed poster of the former

Liverpool footballer, then looks at me. 'He was my hero. He was a legend.'

'Do you play much football yourself?' I ask.

'I used to. I've been playing kickabout with Ross and Ben and another support worker called Jamal. Who is much better than Ben,' he adds.

Ben laughs. 'My man, you are pushing it!'

They both look out of the window. We're lucky to have a large garden and it has a big expanse of grass. I see them looking at the space and suddenly find myself hoping that Diego doesn't want to turn it into a football pitch.

'The park is only ten minutes away by foot and has a brilliant football area,' I say. 'And the football club is right next to your new school, Diego.'

'Good,' Diego says. Then, as if reading my thoughts, 'That means your garden will live, Louise.'

I like him even more!

When we walk back downstairs together, Diego says to Lloyd, 'Thank you for the room. That's really cool what you've done. I really appreciate it.'

'Thank Louise. It was all her doing,' Lloyd says.

Simon looks curious.

'Diego has Liverpool bedding and a big poster of Jota up there,' Ben explains.

Simon thanks me, while Kendi looks sheepish. Diego and Ben head out of the door to the car for their drive.

In their absence, Simon and Ross get down to security. Ross and Ben will be staying up the road in a Travelodge until Sunday afternoon. They will install cameras inside and outside the house.

Hmm. We didn't sign up for that.

'Umm, not cameras inside, thank you,' I say, assuming that will be the end of that.

'Louise is right,' Lloyd agrees. 'It's not appropriate. This is our family home.'

There is a moment of quiet, then Simon says, 'How about just by Diego's room?'

I look at Lloyd and he looks at me. I can tell he is unsure, so I say, 'Okay, Lloyd?'

Lloyd nods.

Ross says that he will fix discreet cameras to all corners of the house, looking in both directions of the street and covering the back entrances from several vantage points. 'Are you happy for us to install a camera doorbell?'

We live in a listed building and some of this really hurts. 'Only while Diego is with us, I suppose?' looking at Lloyd.

He nods again.

'Extra locks will be put on all of the doors and windows for peace of mind,' Ross continues.

Peace of mind? I was actually okay before this little security chat. Now I have no peace of mind.

Simon talks about Diego's 'learnt self-protection skills' and all the training he's had to get to this stage. 'So he is well aware of the security measures that he must abide by at all times.'

Although we know a great deal about the kind of trauma he has suffered, I ask the elephant-in-the-room question.

'Are we allowed to know what actually happened?'

Simon first sits back, presses his fingers together, then leans forward again to speak. 'Diego witnessed a murder between two rival gangs.'

I swallow nervously, and find myself panicking again, trying to keep it on the inside as I ask what he saw.

'He saw another young gang kid get shot and killed.'

I look across at Kendi, who was so unsupportive of me asking for extra funding for this placement. He looks down at the table.

'Yeah,' Simon says. 'It's pretty grim.'

Ross asks me if I am okay.

'Yes, I think. That's awful. But what happened to Diego after?'

'He was obviously terrified, legged it and managed to get away. At the time there was so much commotion the gang didn't notice, but Diego would obviously be able to recognise – and probably name – the elder who did it, as well as identify the other gang members.'

It really is horrible.

'I doubt very much if the young lad who carried out the shooting had a choice. They threaten to kill family members if instructions aren't carried out. And in that world, they go through with their threats.'

I swallow again. We are inviting 'that world' into our home.

They question us about the people who regularly come into our home. Aside from the kids' school friends, there's only Cinnamon, our cleaner, who comes once a week and could be described as 'regular', I think.

'But she's very discreet,' I add. I wouldn't want to be without her. I wouldn't be able to do what I do without her efficient help with the house.

Paperwork is passed over, further arrangements are made. Ben and Diego return. Simon leaves and Ross and Ben go out to the car and begin to install the security devices straightaway.

'How did Simon get back?' I ask, thinking that Simon was the driver of the 4x4.

'Oh, he has a Jag.'

They take out a fold-up ladder from the boot, which is swiftly assembled so they can reach the high spots. Lloyd is very interested; he has never seen one as neat and efficient as that before. I leave him to the devout equipment-worship and ask Diego if he is hungry.

'Well, I wouldn't say no,' Diego says. 'I'd eat if you put food in front of me.'

He has a warm, easy-going personality, and already seems comfortable. I think he will be no problem at all.

'What do you fancy?' I ask, knowing already that I will have most bases covered.

'I've been living on junk food,' he says, making a face of disgust. 'I wouldn't mind some pasta, if you have some.'

I pull a large box of penne out of the cupboard and boil the kettle to fill the pan. Diego sits down near me and chats about this and that. Again, I'm struck by how confident and grown-up he seems. He asks questions about the children while I grab a small onion and a tin of tomatoes from the cupboard, and the red pesto sauce and tomato puree from the fridge. There is some garlic bread in the freezer. I take one out and put the oven as I tell him about the household.

'Vincent likes playing basketball and Jackson has done a bit of rugby but I'm not sure it's his forte. He isn't very good at hurting people. He keeps stopping and apologising.'

Diego finds this funny. 'Do they play football?'

'Not really. Lloyd is the football person. Well, when I say *football person*, I mean he watches it and keeps up with it rather than playing it.'

I tell him that when we lived in Portsmouth, Lloyd had

a season ticket. 'He always moaned, though. They always seemed to lose, week in, week out.'

The pasta is boiling away now. I chop garlic and put it in with the onions and add oregano.

'Good flavours,' Diego says, approvingly.

In goes the puree, followed by the chopped tomatoes. I add a bit of water and let it all cook down to a fine sauce. I add two big spoons of pesto.

'It all smells delicious,' he says, as the different ingredients go in.

The oven is heated and ready and I chuck in the garlic bread.

'Do you like cheese, Diego?'

He nods with an entertaining level of enthusiasm.

I grate a pile of hard cheese and put it in a ramekin. When the garlic bread has browned and the butter is nice and runny I pull it open and pop it on a piece of kitchen roll in a basket. I drain off the pasta and add it to the pan of sauce, mix it in, then transfer it to a pasta bowl. It's simple, but quite the little meal in a short space of time.

Diego looks happy and tucks straight in. There's nothing wrong with his appetite. I get him a large glass of water to go with it and sit opposite him while he eats. I continue chatting about our lives and what we like to do.

Kendi comes in from the garden where all the action with ladders and kit is taking place.

'Louise, do you mind if I have a quick word?'

I hate it when people ask like that. I always think I'm in trouble.

'Back in a sec, Diego. Help yourself if you want more.'

I follow Kendi out to the hall and stand opposite him by the front door.

'Louise, I just wanted to apologise for my recent behaviour. It's not an excuse, but I applied for a manager's role. I was shortlisted and I was trying to make a good impression with my bosses, but then I realised what that was doing and what it would mean. I decided not to go any further with my application after I took on board the full implications: that it would mean not helping the children properly. And, as you clearly noticed, I was distancing myself a little from the carers and the children. So, again, I'm sorry.'

It explains a lot.

'And, I shall, in the strongest terms, be asking for an uplift with the allowance on your behalf.'

I thank him. 'I'm glad to have you back on side, Kendi.'

He is not manager material. He will not consent to the metaphorical full frontal lobotomy that I suspect so many middle managers have to have. In order to do their job they must have to forget what it's like at the coalface to keep the senior managers happy. That's not for Kendi. I don't tell him so. It seems he's worked it out for himself.

Ross and Ben come through the back door with Lloyd and comment on the delicious smell in the kitchen. Diego has washed up his pasta bowl and left it draining on the side. This is a great start. Perhaps he'll be able to teach the others a thing or two about clearing up after themselves. He asks if he can go to his room.

'Help yourself,' I say. 'You'll find the remote for the TV behind it on the cabinet.'

He takes himself off upstairs.

'Right. Whose phone and laptop will be connected to the cameras?' Ross asks.

'Lloyd's,' I say, firmly. It would fry my brain to have that level of minutiae going on, all connected to my computer.

Once everything's installed, I stand by them as they show each camera view.

'Oh, I like this! I shall be able to see whose cat comes in and poops in my flowerpots.'

This is clearly not the level of surveillance they had in mind.

'Every time someone comes near the front door, and anywhere around the front, sides and back of the house, Lloyd's phone will sound,' Ross explains, 'enabling you to check who it is and what's going on.'

I'm glad we've gone for Lloyd's devices to house the tech. All that pinging would drive me insane.

'Anything untoward, you contact us immediately,' Ben adds.

'Good luck, Lloyd,' I say.

Ross and Ben are gone before the children are home from school. Diego hides away upstairs in his room. He's been so confident with the adults. I think it's funny how children are more nervous about meeting other children than anyone else.

The boys are back first. Lily messages to say that she is meeting her friend outside Home Bargains and won't be back for a while.

Jackson and Vincent are in the middle of their usual raid of the kitchen when Diego appears at the kitchen door.

'Alright?' says Diego.

Good on him for making the first move.

Within minutes, all the boys are in the sitting room together, gaming. Diego is not allowed a device alone in his room and we can monitor the one in the sitting room.

Lloyd is enjoying his role of surveillance operative. He's like the Fat Controller from *Thomas the Tank Engine* with eyes on us all. Well, not quite – I know where the cameras are.

But what a day.

I feel utterly worn out.

And I have no idea what's yet to come.

IV

I can't sleep.

I am worrying about Diego and the safety of our home. I really wish I hadn't seen *Top Boy*, the TV series set on an East London housing estate that follows the tension between different drug gangs and how characters get drawn in. I've found bits of it really tense, and now can't help feeling that a similar thing is going to play out in our home.

I lie awake, thinking about how I could save each child if we were under attack. Would we call 999? Or run out onto the street screaming? What would happen to Doug? Would a gang shoot him because he barked? I hate being awake in the early hours of the morning. My brain goes into catastrophe mode. *We're all going to die…*

I think I finally manage to nod off at about 5am and, when I wake up, guess what? I'm alive. We're all alive. There have been no murders or shootings. The children are still asleep and Lloyd's snoring is enough to put any criminals off their stride. My panic-brain has achieved nothing more than a desperate need for a strong coffee to get me through the day.

I sit with Doug in the quiet of the morning and smile at how over-reactive I've been. Once the coffee is in my system, I unload the dishwasher. This won't be the last time today. I think I worked out that I do it, on average, four times a day. Once it's empty, I pack all the plates, bowls and pans which the fairies have evidently used in the night inside it, and get it going again. I seriously wonder if the children are coming downstairs during the night to cook and eat? I don't understand where it all comes from otherwise. What is going on?

My catastrophising brain now worries about tea towels on the hob and whether they turn the gas off. Will the house burn down?

This, I suspect, is simply what living with children does to you.

I soak the remaining yoghurt containers, plus the empty jam jar and well-scraped chocolate-spread jar in warm water in the sink. That last is a *difficult* product to soak. Chocolate spread as a chemical compound must be almost indestructible; it certainly doesn't want to come away from the glass jar. I get the brush and attack it. As I look up and out of the kitchen window, I see the well-known neighbourhood big, ginger bully of a tomcat come into our garden. He is vile. We currently have three cats and this is their home. Nevertheless, he bullies them in the garden. *Their* garden. I stand and watch for a minute and wonder if he is stopping, or will he pass through into another garden.

I like most animals, but I think I hate this one. He's built like a brick shithouse, as the saying goes. I can see his muscles ripple with every step. He's like a different species to Fergus, Jackson's black and white cat, who has such a high-pitched squeak he can't even seem to meow properly. Fergus is a sweetie who loves to be cuddled, and this brute targets him.

I look back down at the sink and finish trying to remove stubborn traces of chocolate spread from the jar before I put it in the recycling. I like to rinse all the recycling so that there is nothing sticky or smelly that could mess up the process. When I look back up, the ginger thug has gone. Good.

I gather the plastic and glass from the drainer and move towards the conservatory door to put the recycling out. There's a flash of fur. I look down and the ginger thug-cat is coming through the backdoor cat flap.

The cheeky bugger.

I am furious, partly because I now know why the conservatory smells of cat pee. It's him with his huge, clanking testicles, squirting my home. I put the recycling on the tumble drier and turn to take him on.

He does not run back out of the cat flap; he fronts me out.

I stand and stare at him and call him all the names under the sun, to no effect. He does not move. In fact, he looks like he is going to eat me.

Suddenly Diego appears and sees the stand-off. He runs up to the ginger thug-monster and claps his hands. 'Back off, you!'

The monster cat looks at us with an expression that says, 'Maybe not this time, but *next time* I'm going to get you!' before slinking away.

I thank Diego for his timely intervention.

He laughs. 'Oh, he was easy: he didn't have a gun.'

I look at him sharply, not knowing if I should smile at that remark or not. I do. Not least because I'm picturing the cat returning with a cat-sized machine gun and bullets slung over one shoulder.

'What would you like for breakfast, Diego?'

'Whatever's going,' he says with a grin.

'Okay, well in that case, would you like egg, bacon and the whole shebang?'

He beams and nods. I go to the freezer to get the hash browns. Within a minute or two of the bacon hitting the frying pan, Vincent appears.

'Morning, Diego.'

I ask Vincent if he'd like a cooked breakfast and he is

keen, too. The boys sit down with orange juice and talk about gaming.

Then Jackson comes in, although not for breakfast. He doesn't really eat with us anymore. Since he started college and the gym he has taken to a high-protein diet, telling us that his body is a temple.

It isn't, because I see all the chocolate and sweet wrappers in his bedroom bin, but hey, if that's his story, I'll go with it. We've had to start spending a small fortune on coconut water, protein bars that look to me like sweets, and packets of 'creatine' powder, whatever that might be. I have no idea, but this stuff seems to cost more than all of our food. Still, it seems to be working for him. He certainly knows his stuff. This is where schools get it wrong. Jackson didn't really engage properly with much when he was still in school, because he wasn't that interested. But get him on the subject of fitness and healthy eating and he could give you a full-length lecture without referring to his notes.

It's early days, but the boys all seem to get on well, despite Diego being the youngest by a couple of years. It's his confidence and air of being much older, I think.

He tells me he was the 'man of his house'. I can't tell if he says it with pride or bitterness, but it's an interesting phrase and I would love to hear more about it in due course. It can wait for now. When the time is right, I'll return to it.

'So, why are you boys all up so early at the weekend?'

'Got an appointment,' Vincent says. 'Gaming,' he says, when I look confused. 'No time to waste. Got to get on.'

Jackson is going to the gym regularly. I have never seen him as disciplined and motivated as he is at the moment. It's paying off, because he does look great. Oodles better than when he was at school.

The three young men talk about fitness and health. Diego asks if he can join a local gym. He's a bit too young, but the school where he is going has a gym that students can use. It's shared with the community.

'I just need all the confirmations from school and then I'll book you in,' I tell him.

Diego asks if the boys fancy playing a bit of football.

'Yeah, cool,' Vincent says.

Jackson also nods agreement.

'Do you have a football?' I ask them.

They don't know – which should probably give Diego a clue about their playing ability.

Lloyd walks in, looking for his coffee cup. He is ready for another, but sees the plates and smells the bacon, which gives him an even better idea.

'Oh, can I have some egg and bacon, too?'

I feel like I'm running a greasy spoon café. Or I might as well be.

'And I'll go and look for the football,' Lloyd says.

I don't hold out much hope. I haven't seen one for ages. Not since Vincent kicked it into our old neighbour's garden. He was a hateful, grumpy man, who probably stabbed it with his devil's trident.

I throw a couple more rashers into the frying pan. While I'm cooking Lloyd's breakfast, he heads down to the shed but comes back after a few minutes, empty-handed.

'Perhaps after breakfast we can head into town – to that independent sports shop, you know the one I mean – and get a new ball,' I say. My suggestion is well-received.

When Jackson is back from the gym, and we have the new ball, they head over to the park.

I love this.

Just the fact of getting on with a new foster child is always a relief. But I love it when the children hit it off and drive the activities together. It's just the best thing to see.

I haven't seen Lily yet. I wonder what she's up to. Eventually she comes downstairs and it's clear what she's been up to. She is sporting fully washed, dried and straightened hair, and is wearing tight jeans and a crop top.

I almost spill my coffee.

She looks rather 'overdone', especially for home, but who cares when she is trying out a new look.

'Wow, Lily, you look stunning.'

She shrugs like it's no big deal and then casually asks where the boys are.

Ah, I think I'm cottoning on. 'Which boy?'

She blushes.

This is an interesting development, not least because for the last few months Lily has been gay.

Or has she? I'm not sure I've got that right? I get confused. Since we looked after Sparkle, our LGBTQi child, the goal posts have moved again.

Lily today, is exploiting what nature gave her in ways that might be considered under the 'male gaze'. I'm sure she's put socks in her bra. When did she become so busty?

She seems to deflate a little at discovering that Diego has gone to the park, which rather confirms my suspicion that Lady Lily might have a bit of a crush on Diego, even though she's in the school year above him. She won't appreciate it if I call her a 'cradle snatcher' though, so I resist the temptation.

I have promised to stay in daily contact with Ross and Ben, so I make the call. I grew rather fond of them over the several hours they were here installing equipment that I'm sure wouldn't have seemed out of place in an episode of *Spooks*.

I get through to Ben and report on the apparent success of Diego's first night here. I tell him about the boys all going to the park, and how I'm genuinely impressed with how the boys are getting on with Diego.

'But he is so mature which probably helps. And explains why I keep thinking he's older than he is.'

Ross is in the background and makes a quip about age not mattering on the football pitch and not fancying my boys' chances against the fancy-footwork of Diego.

Ross and Ben are quite the double act and I can't imagine them ever not working together.

'Well, there was a time you wouldn't have said that,' Ben tells me. He then explains that while they get on now and genuinely enjoy each other's company, they were once in opposing gangs.

'There was a time when I thought Ross was the enemy. Until Simon changed all that. I met Simon ten years ago, when he first set up Freeedom. I was still a teenager, probably a similar age to Diego. Simon arranged for us both to meet. We didn't actually know that we were going to meet, or it would never have happened. But Simon's a canny bastard.'

'What did he do?' I ask, intrigued.

'Me and Ben were driven, separately, to a village hall in the middle of bloody nowhere. I remember it well. It didn't look like anything was going on there and I had no idea what was gonna happen. Simon turned up in his flash Jag. The worker I was with walked me into the hall. I thought he was just another gang member, but he became my mentor, afterwards, actually. Anyway, he walked me into the hall and Ross had someone with him, doing the same thing. I recognised him from a rival gang. We sat down and Simon walked in. He was like a guru,' Ben laughs.

'Basically, he asked us both a load of questions like, what's your favourite music, food, clothes, what sort of school did you go to.'

'In front of each other?'

'Yeah, and when we gave our answers, he carefully pointed out that we had more in common than not and he spent a good deal of time explaining how dark crime rings work, how they divide to rule.'

It strikes me that Simon and his fellow workers are like modern-day superheroes, using their powers to help the world become a better place, protecting the public and fighting crime.

Ben laughs again when I tell him that. 'You're not wrong. I remember Simon explaining the hierarchy of it all. How, above the elders in the gang are their bosses and above them are bigger bosses, and so on. County lines is like a tall, pointy pyramid with people at the top that look like they're good. They might even be in government, or the police, or business, or media or whatever. They can be anywhere and everywhere. When Simon explained how we were both being exploited and showed us how we could get out, we believed him and haven't looked back.'

I wonder how many kids like Ben and Ross, and now Diego, Freeedom has helped over the years. They have a network of agents across the country who can jump in at any time to help. There is something cult-like about Freeedom, but in a good way. They know what they are doing.

I ask Ben how many young people are involved in county lines.

'We don't know. No one knows for sure, because the reporting is so hard. Recording numbers and converting that into proper data relies on no corruption. And that's not something we can depend on.'

I find this fascinating and report the whole conversation back to Lloyd. He is in his office looking at the many screens. It must be like living in the White House with a top security detail round the clock. I see something out of place on one: a dangerous cat. I work out where the mean, lairy, ginger tom, thug-brute cat is, and head out with a cup of water to throw at him. If nothing else, the cameras are good for teaching this nasty boy a lesson and keeping him out of our garden and house.

My phone goes. It's Kendi, and today, I am much happier to speak to him. I have moved on from feeling like he was a traitor, poacher-turned-gamekeeper.

'Hi Kendi, how are you?'

'I'm good, Louise, very good, and I have some good news, too.'

That's more like the Kendi I enjoy working with. 'Oh, good. Go on.'

'I've been in touch with Diego's local authority and they recognise that this is not a standard placement, exactly as you put it. They have offered an uplift to your fee, of £100 per week.'

That's £400 per month, not an insignificant sum, and much better than nothing. As a foster carer we will always say, 'better than nothing' because so often 'nothing' is exactly what we get. I'm pleased about the uplift, but it would also have been nice if they had acknowledged it at the beginning, without us having to chase. We shouldn't have to ask for danger money.

After the stab of vindication, I feel bad about asking.

Then I remind myself that this is how it works. Too often foster carers wear meek little cardigans and are too scared to hold up our begging bowls.

When I go to meetings or meet people and say 'I'm an author' they look at me and smile and genuinely want to know more. When I say, 'I'm the CEO of a charity', that also sparks interest. But if I start with, 'I'm a foster carer' most seem to ignore me, because being a woman and a foster carer means being a frump and a bore. Or I get the, 'Oh, you must be a saint, I don't know how you do it.'

Men get a bit more credibility, I think. I wish the system would help change our image. Because we are mostly women on low, or no, fee, we have no employment rights and no voice. We are the epitome of 'wimmins work.' I won't say that to Lloyd, because I'm moving closer to getting him to load and unload the dishwasher and I don't want to sabotage years of hard work over something as silly as women's rights – never mind foster carers' rights.

The boys come back from the park having lost the ball. I tell them it doesn't matter: an additional £400 a month will keep us bountifully supplied with new footballs!

V

Ross or Ben call every day and Simon calls every other day. They like to speak to Diego when they can. After a week, there is nothing very much to report, other than we have now documented evidence that a ginger tom is traumatising our cats and stealing their food.

I have looked up 'gang murders' in Liverpool and can't seem to find anything. I have actually spent far too much time on the internet trying to find any crimes in Liverpool that have taken place in the last year that could be the crime associated with Diego and what he witnessed.

I confess to Simon. Although I can't see him over the phone, I sense the smile in his voice as he tells me that it didn't take place in Liverpool.

'They're clever. They don't want the association on their turf. So, no, I'm afraid you won't find out any more.'

So it could have happened literally anywhere in the country. Oh, this is frustrating. How am I meant to research this? I realise that the point is that I'm *not* meant to research it, but I can't help but be curious. I wonder if

I can ask him directly. I decide against it. It would feel like a step too far, crossing a boundary. He is not meant to talk about it and I should not ask. That way we all stay safe.

I ask Diego what he would most like for dinner. He is always very compliant and eats anything I put in front of him. Each day he has endured all *our* choices with perfect grace and politeness. But there's no better hospitality than serving someone their favourite food, so I press him.

'If you could have anything at all, what would it be?'

He thinks about it for a bit and then says, 'It would have to be lasagne, or bacalhau.'

'Bacalhow?'

'It's a Portuguese dish. A salt cod stew.'

I can make lasagne any day and, actually, Lloyd makes a fantastic lasagne. Everyone likes it. Apart from Jackson, and that's only a recent development, since he comes in and cooks his weird protein food with six eggs washed down with coconut water, leaving the kitchen looking as if we have been burgled by a gang of food-hating maniacs. Although Jackson denies making any mess.

Now we have the thug-cat caught on camera, every single misdemeanour that takes place in the house is being blamed on feline activity. It's become something of a game.

'Somebody's opened the biscuits and left them out.'

'It's probably that big ginger tom.'

'Somebody's left dripping wet towels on the bathroom floor. Again.'

'Yeah, I reckon it's that cat.'

'Who didn't hang their coat up?'

'I did, but that cat knocked it off again.'

I digress. I'll happily make a lasagne, but I'm intrigued to hear more about this cod stew.

Diego tells me his mama would make it sometimes on a Saturday.

'It's salted cod, sweet onions, eggs and olives. We had it with fresh bread and then she served creamy rice pudding, made with loads of eggs, with a crispy sugar on top.'

I must admit this sounds gorgeous, particularly the pudding. Who knows, with that amount of eggs in it, maybe Jackson would eat it.

'I'll do some research,' I promise.

First, I need to get Diego some uniform. He'll start school in a week's time. He will be going to the same school as Lily and Vincent, who are both in the upper years. So a uniform is my next job.

Until not so long ago, there was a wonderful family business that stocked the uniform here in the town. It was a rite of passage for so many children. I remember taking the boys in – and so many foster children over the years – to get fitted for their blazers and pick up their sports kits and football socks. It was part of the routine and a way of helping the children get ready for school. But last year, the school decided to stop using the family business that had served the school and community for several generations, and instead they went with an online school uniform provider. A company that seems, for reasons best known to themselves, to manufacture blazers with absurdly long arms. I had to turn up the cuffs for Lily and Vincent last year, they were so long they nearly covered their knuckles. I thought at first that it was my children who were freakishly short-armed, but when I went into school and had the chance to observe the other children, they all had overlong sleeves. It made them all look like they were in dressing-up clothes. Without the trade from the local school, the family business went bust. The shop still stands empty: yet another hit for a community trying to keep its high street alive. I browse the online shop and seriously hope it gets here by Friday, but the website says their lead time is five to nine working days. I'm so glad they killed off the service that *actually worked.*

School shoes we'll have to do in person, though I don't know how much joy we'll have. Along with the uniform outfitters, there was always a mad dash to the big town to buy shoes which became cut-throat because, if you went too soon, their feet could still grow, and if you left it too late most of the shoes had sold out. Somewhere around the 18th of August was always my target date. We'd head out early, first to Clarks, because even though they didn't always love the shoes, it somehow gave the children a weird sense of worth and sent the message that 'they are loved'. Then we'd head to the other shoe shops to go for whatever was left. It was like a military operation that required coffee and possibly paracetamol. I would always say one pair of school shoes, one pair of trainers for sport, and one pair of mucking about shoes. Once, I took six children and it cost hundreds of pounds. That came with an added shock, because the local authority for those siblings suddenly announced that it no longer did a uniform allowance. Consequently, we worked for 'free' for about three weeks that summer.

I do a bit of web-browsing and discover that there is a Portuguese food shop in the big town. It's a little bit further to drive than I would usually go for food shopping, but needs must. I load up with a lot of stuff. I buy 20 'pastel de nata' (that's custard tarts to most of us) alongside other biscuits and sweets. I buy jars of piri piri sauces and tins of sardines. We could all do with a bit more Omega 3 oil. Lloyd is a bit shocked when I tell him that I ended up spending over £80.

'But I want Diego to feel at home,' I protest. I get the impression 'home' was a good place, or at least it was once, and anything we can do to help him settle in has to be valuable.

'And, if we eat a Mediterranean diet, we'll all feel – and be – much healthier.'

I've also bought a couple of terracotta pots for cooking and hope that it reminds Diego of better days. They are beautiful, from a little stall in the market.

I plan to wait until Saturday to make Diego's special dinner, since that was the day he told me that his mum used to make it.

Predictably, the blazer does not arrive by Friday. I spend the morning phoning the company and being put on hold, which sends me through the roof. I have kept Vincent's old blazer, so Diego can go in that for a few days, but this is not how I wanted it to be for him. Children in care deserve some dignity and for me, being in county lines and seeing a murder is right up there with the worst kinds of child abuse. I want to show this child some respect but, as always in this world of fostering and children's social care, 'better than nothing' is our standard.

On Saturday morning I'm greeted in the kitchen by a bright-eyed and bushy-tailed Diego and Vincent, both requiring a cooked breakfast before they play football in the park. Jackson breezes in with his gym clothes on and they all high five and knuckle hello. The latter is new. I do my best to keep up, but I don't expect I shall be required to partake in this particular greeting.

Jackson says that he will meet them down the park

after his session at the gym. It's like a repeat of the previous weekend.

Lloyd comes into the kitchen, clearly led once again by the smell of frying bacon. 'What's everyone up to today?' he asks.

The children seem to have all become fitter and sportier in the space of a few weeks. In comes Lily, in a tracksuit that I have no memory of ever seeing before. She heads to get a banana from the fruit bowl and then casually says, 'I'm off for my run.'

Have I just woken up in someone else's house?

It's not just the children, because Lloyd then completely freaks me out. 'I'm going for a cycle.'

He has not touched that £2,000 carbon racing bike I bought him 12 years ago for his birthday in as long as I can remember. He had all the gear and less than no idea. But suddenly, my family has turned into the Brownlee brothers, it seems. Perhaps I should be searching out the Lycra, too.

I dish up breakfast, wave off Bradley Wiggins and watch them all merrily disperse into this theatre of health and wellbeing.

I shake my head and mutter away to Doug while I stack the dishwasher. He is as shocked as I am. Or at least that's how I'm interpreting the fact that he has his head cocked to one side.

After loading the dishwasher, I put in the first load of washing and turn them both on. Lloyd, currently busy doing his best Chris Froome impression, is not here to say 'you can't have the dishwasher and washing machine on at the same time' and I feel a gleeful sense of subversion as I turn the dial.

I sweep up the biscuits Doug knocked out of his bowl, and brush away the tsunami of crumbs and mess the children seem to have covered the floor with this morning. The reality is that the kitchen floor needs a sweep more than once a day, but once a day is all I can manage and so that is what it gets. I'm rather fond of our old, wooden, tall dustpan and brush – it was hand-crafted by a visually-impaired group who meet in the town and make things to sell.

Chores complete, I take Doug out for a little stroll around the other park – I don't want the boys to think I'm checking up on their training session – so he can meet some of his canine chums. He is missing Dotty dreadfully, and some mornings he still stands in the garden and howls, but he doesn't seem to be quite so dedicated to this practice as he was in the early stages of his grief. Certainly, if it's raining, he doesn't bother. I take this to mean that he is healing. But, nevertheless, he enjoys the company of other dogs.

I don't tell Diego that my day will be spent cooking

him a Portuguese dinner for tonight. I don't want to put him, or me, under any pressure. It could go horribly wrong. I found the recipes online and, as always, there are different versions. I go for the ones which purport to be the most 'traditional' for both the main and the pudding. I am prepared with all the ingredients I need, apart from the salt cod – which is at the fish counter of Waitrose in the next town. Another 16-mile drive there and back. Why did I start this! I think positively, assume that the cooking will go well, and decide to buy some extra for the freezer.

Lloyd is back quite quickly from his evidently not-so-long-distance bicycle ride. I choose not to tell him that he looks like a shiny tomato and should not have worn a red cycling top since it's hard to tell where the Lycra ends and his neck starts. He sits on the bench by the window, his helmet on the floor, holding his bike with one hand. The other hand is up as a stop sign to me.

'Are you okay?'

He can hardly breathe.

'I'll be alright in a minute,' he gasps.

I go back indoors. His phone is pinging because he is sitting in sight of a camera and I have just walked past another one. Ping, ping. Even after a couple of weeks, I'm still not entirely used to it. But I do my best to ignore it and lay out the recipes. I start with the rice pudding, because it seems more complicated than the dinner.

I have a lovely Saturday.

Is it enhanced by the fact that Lloyd can hardly speak after his exertions?

The lads are in the park kicking a ball about.

Lily is out with her friends, probably circling the park would be my guess. Louise 'Sherlock' Allen saw that they had all straightened their hair and done their make-up like they're heading to a nightclub in order to go 'for a walk'.

Doug lies in his bed while I bring him little tasters as I cook. Like a king, he just lifts his head, sniffs and decides to accept the proffered morsel, then puts his head back down and waits until I return to wait on him again.

I prepare the meal in the new Portuguese pottery ware and feel pretty damn pleased with myself. There may even be some whistling while I work. Certainly some singing along to the radio.

The showers are busy when the boys get back. All I hear, aside from the thundering up and down stairs and along the hallway from bathroom to bedrooms is, 'I'm starving, what's for dinner?'

I have three tear-and-share breads of different varieties, also from Waitrose, so no one will go hungry.

Vincent is first down, clean, fresh and straight into a moan about Lily and her dorky friends. 'Mum, can you tell Lily to fuck off?'

I say that the answer to that question is a definite no.

Vincent's hormones have made him a bit grumpy and lacking in patience. Jackson thinks it's hilarious and winds him up even more.

'What's the problem with Lily and her friends walking around the park? It's a free country, you know, and that's a public space.'

I know absolutely what the problem is and why he's annoyed. He thinks they are stupid and 'irrelevant' which seems to be the current insult of choice. But, being Vincent, he would not want to lower the tone of the game and tell them that in public.

Before Diego comes down to join us, both Vincent and Jackson remark on how good he is at football. They are *very* impressed.

'I think because Diego is settling in and finding his feet, his confidence showed through on the field,' Jackson comments.

Somebody give this man a job on *Match of the Day.* He sounds exactly like one of the pundits.

A minute later, Diego comes in wearing his clean grey tracksuit and white Nike high socks. He smells of Lynx. Oh, I hate that smell. I make a mental note to take him to Superdrug and get him to choose a new smell, one that I find a little less toxic.

My moment has arrived.

The whole crew is sitting around the table, even Jackson, for once, and I think that's because he's enjoying the vibe of the evening. I place the bread down first, then a big salad with seeds on top, and then I bring out the bacalhau with a flourish.

'Ta da!'

Diego lights up and claps his hands together.

'My favourite! I thought I smelt it, but I didn't think it could be.'

The food is appreciated by all and eaten with gusto, apart from Lily who suddenly decides that she has an issue with cod, until Diego talks about the meals in Portugal and then she shuts up and tucks in, too.

I note the adoring way she gazes at him, and share a look with Lloyd, who has spotted it too. He is rather dashing. They all are, but Jackson and Vincent have been her foster brothers for years. Diego, on the other hand, is a superstar of great mystery.

He is open and talks about his mum, whom he very sweetly calls his 'mama', and his dad, and what happened during the pandemic. He says that the troubles started before that, though, and because of Brexit.

Lloyd is first in with his views on Brexit, swiftly followed by Vincent, whose views are roughly the same but with more swearing.

Jackson, who is doing politics as one of his A-levels

at college, is a little more circumspect, and refers to the propaganda around the campaign. 'It played on ignorance and fear,' he says, with the assured wisdom of a teenager.

Lily's contribution is perhaps the most surprising. I'd forgotten she actually has a brain with all the time spent on padded chicken-liver bras, hair and make-up of late.

'Did you know that the protesters in the right wing who parasite causes such as violence against girls and who try to turn it into a race issue, over half are on record for domestic violence?'

No, I did not know this and I don't know where Lily is getting her information from, but I'm pleased that she has a view. Typical Allen dinner: never light and polite conversation, but straight to the nub of things. Unless Nan, Lloyd's mum, turns up for dinner. In which case the rules change and we resort to light and polite in deference to her.

The conversation moves on. Diego talks about the dark crime rings and how vulnerable young men are manipulated, and the role that social media plays in it all. I ask Diego if he knows about Andrew Tate.

His reply is pretty short and direct: 'Yeah, wanker.'

Then he apologises for swearing.

Andrew Tate has been the subject of many a discussion in the Allen household. Diego claims that we are all being used and manipulated to help make people like Tate rich.

He mentions various politicians, here and abroad, and it's clear he doesn't shy away from having an opinion.

I ask if he thinks that gang culture is influenced by Andrew Tate.

This takes slightly longer to think about. 'Yeah, it is, but mostly just the white boys. We're all being exploited, but they're too stupid to see it.'

I think the world has gone mad. They really are trying to cause division in this country – and even inside gangs and within gang-culture there are layers of weirdness. I feel pleased that the food has gone down so well, that there is a healthy level of debate around the table and that we are raising young people with well-considered opinions who aren't afraid to share them.

There is no sign of any trouble, and I think we made the right decision in inviting Diego into our home.

VI

On Monday morning, Diego heads out to school with Vincent, wearing Vincent's old blazer.

'Don't worry,' Diego assures me when I apologise. 'It's actually better that it's not new. First of all, I'm used to it. And anyway, I'd stick out even more with a brand new one.'

Perhaps the new one, when it arrives, might be sent straight back.

Lily is not far behind her foster brothers. She is desperate to walk with Vincent and Diego, but Vincent is equally insistent that is *not* suddenly going to start happening.

Lloyd and I get on with our day, both working from home. As ever, I have loads of work to catch up on. I can hear Lloyd's phone pinging. I look out of the window and see that the alert is actually caused by Doug going for a wee.

Then, about an hour later, I hear a raised voice. 'You evil little shit!'

I leap up and wonder why Lloyd is talking to Doug this way. What on earth has Doug done?! I arrive in the kitchen to see Lloyd dashing out to the garden with an empty tin from the recycling box. The big ginger tom has Mabel on the floor and is attacking her. Doug is barking his head off and Lloyd is furious. The cat jumps off Mabel, who is seriously scratched. Lloyd throws the can at the tom cat, who is so unfazed as he slouches off, he might as well have turned and stuck his middle finger up at us.

It sounds ridiculous, but I'm actually beginning to feel a little threatened by this cat.

I decide that I'll wait until the next time the nasty beast is about and remember to take his photo.

'I'll put him on Facebook and see if he is traumatising other residents and their lives,' I tell Lloyd.

When Diego and Vincent get home, I tell them about the evil tom cat. They are both hungry, so I make them a bagel with ham and cheese to keep them going, with the necessary addition of a gherkin and mayonnaise.

'So, how was your day, Diego? Did everything go okay?' I ask.

Diego puts down his bagel and sits back in his chair. 'Well, the school has county lines, clear as day, but the teachers are blind to it.'

I love his rich, Liverpudlian accent. It sounds so expressive.

'What makes you think that?'

'You can tell. Poor kids with flash trainers. Or rich ones with busy parents who speak posher, but are already in deep. The girls looking for a bit of love and attention. You can just see it.'

'But what in particular?' I persist.

'Language. You can tell who knows what they're talking about by the words they use.'

'Don't all teenagers use the same sort of slang?'

'They do and they don't,' Diego says, enigmatically. 'There's the wannabe pretenders, all gob and no real idea, and there's the real thing. But I'm telling you county lines is in the school.'

Vincent shrugs, like he knows too and none of this is news. I'm not surprised. It's everywhere. Simon has made that clear. We might consider ourselves to live in a nice part of the world and enjoy our Waitrose shopping, but that doesn't mean there isn't a trap line running beneath our noses.

'Are you worried by it?' I ask.

'No. They don't know me, and I plan to keep my head down.'

'But if you can tell who knows what they're talking about, won't they be able to tell the same about you?' Sherlock Allen is back.

'I can look after meself,' Diego says.

He looks and sounds as if he can, too. He almost seems older than Vincent. But still, I have a little shiver of foreboding.

I take the dog out for a stroll the following afternoon. I'm trying to encourage Doug to take some interest in life again, meet other dogs and people. Dogs definitely suffer from grief and theirs might be a purer form than ours, not mixed up with money, power and games as ours so often is.

Given Dotty's sudden demise, I'm keeping a close eye on Doug, and I have to say that I think he's looking in pretty good shape, despite the extra ounces. I have instructed everyone – including me – not to feed him any extras, though not everyone is following these instructions – especially me – as the weekend's cooking demonstrates. It's the eyes. How can you resist the eyes?

'He can have a carrot,' I say, when the kids try to feed him titbits. I must try harder to follow my own rules.

My dog walk has coincided with school chucking out time. I walk behind children I have known for years who look like adults now. I used to see them walk past the window when they were little. Now they are tall and hairy and the girls walk with wiggles. There's nothing like seeing little kids become adults to make you realise the way the blasted clock keeps ticking. I realise I am actually, inadvertently, walking behind Diego, who has put his hoodie over his blazer, and is wearing it with the hood up.

I hang back a bit. I don't want to embarrass him. But I watch. He's not shifty, exactly, but he's careful. He is definitely watching every car and every person that goes by. He is a little jumpy. Perhaps that's hardly surprising. His walk to and from school must be stressful for him. However confident and articulate he presents, the poor boy has post-traumatic stress. There must be some support available for him, surely? Seeing him out 'in the wild' like this reminds me that he needs it, and I should chase this up with Kendi and Simon. I know Simon said that they can't expose information to CAMHS or other agencies, but there must be a private counsellor, who doesn't need to know his real name? It's true that you can't ignore the Liverpudlian accent, and it sticks out around here, but Liverpool is a big city with more than half a million inhabitants. That figure trebles if you take in the wider Liverpool region. A bit smaller than Manchester. Still, a big enough number to get lost in. It *must* be possible to get him some treatment.

Poor boy.

I watch him as he gets towards the front door. He looks all ways first to see if it's safe. It must be really hard to live your life like that, on constant alert. He knocks at the door. We were advised to not give him a key, just in case it got into the wrong hands. But I can guarantee that no one will let him in. Lloyd is out and those teenagers avoid answering the door because they're big babies and don't want to deal with what might be beyond it. They pretend not to hear it, in exactly the same way as they pretend not to notice that the toilet roll is running out, leaving just one sheet on the brown cardboard tube so that they don't have to deal with it. If I ask them about why they didn't open the front door they will all say, 'I didn't hear it.'

Jackson came back from the gym the other day and had forgotten his key. Everyone was out apart from me. He knocked on the door. I thought Lloyd was in, so I left it. The knocking became louder and louder and more and more insistent. I wondered if it was a drugged-up delivery man, but no, it was my own son, red-faced and extremely angry.

'Why didn't you let me in?' he demanded.

'I didn't hear it,' I said with a look of wide-eyed 'innocence', knowing that the same phrase is usually offered by those of the teenage persuasion.

I don't want Diego to have to wait to be let in. It's bad enough that he can't have a key. I call out to him while he stands on the doorstep, looking around awkwardly.

His face immediately breaks out into a wide smile, any trace of anxiety gone. 'Alright, Louise?'

When I listen to Diego I find myself thinking of John

Lennon. But I am an accent thief. If I'm in the company of anyone with an accent, I steal it, often without realising. It must be so annoying for them, and I barely notice that I'm doing it.

'Alright?' I say back, sounding like a character in *Brookside*.

It's not even a word I would usually use as a greeting, 'alright', but the copycat accent is impossible to resist.

Diego wants to play football, as he always seems to, and it's the first thing he asks Vincent when he gets home a few minutes later. While they dash upstairs to get changed, I make them bagels and offer them a bag of Nik Naks each, operating under the belief, probably false, that corn-based snacks have to be marginally healthier than ordinary crisps.

In comes Lily with her mate, Ellie.

'The boys are getting changed,' I say. 'What are you two up to?'

They look at each other and smirk. No answer is forthcoming, so I can guess.

The boys come down in tracksuit bottoms, trainers and t-shirts, all trace of one uniform substituted for another.

The girls blush.

Vincent walks past them and doesn't realise that I overhear his whispered, 'losers', directed at them.

I will let him off for now so I don't embarrass him, but make a mental note to bring that one back up later.

The boys wolf down their snack and head off with goalkeeping gloves and the ball. The girls look at each other and dart upstairs. Half an hour later they reappear, hair remarkably straighter than when they went up, and now both dressed in Lily's outfits.

'Where are you two going?'

They shrug and head out of the door.

'Dinner is at 7pm,' I call after them.

They will see him at dinner time, I'm sure. As well as in the street and at the park. I can see that young Diego has attracted a lot of attention from the girls. Not just Lily and her friend, there are another two waiting outside. I watch them all walk along the road, trying to pretend that they aren't chasing off after the boys.

I smile to myself, remembering when I would walk around the village where I grew up, along with my best mate, the pair of us flicking our hair as we walked past the boys playing football. Although I also remember becoming quite bored of this activity very quickly because, actually, why weren't *we* playing football? My taste in boys went 'alternative' when I first heard punk and new wave. Duran Duran's *Planet Earth* turned my head away from the sporty jocks and towards boys in make-up and their mums' favourite blouses.

It's all such a long time ago now, but still fresh in the memory.

Diego is creating new waves of his own.

I'd love to know what his real name is, but that's totally against the rules. He is an enigma, and watching the girls fawn over him is fascinating. Vincent and Jackson seem to behave in ways that are almost protective of him – protecting him from the girls, at least. In the grand scheme of things, when I think about what this poor kid has been through in such a short time, I'm sure he would be able to handle himself in that department, but it's interesting to see.

'There is a match on TV tonight, have you heard?' Diego beams when they come back, just in time for dinner.

I haven't heard, but I think I'm about to.

'Liverpool versus Man City.'

The boys all cheer and Lloyd is made up. He has already been to the shops and has everything a football fan would want ready for the game, apart from the tins of lager. He will be drinking wine.

There are various crisps and nibbles, plus biscuits and a giant bag of popcorn; everything in place ready for the 8pm kick-off.

It's probably at this point that it would be wise to make a confession: I have never really sat through a football match, in its entirety, before. I also need to make it known that Lloyd and the boys never played football together, either. I'm not even sure if the boys were interested before

Diego's arrival, but it's endearing to watch this play out before me.

I have no clue what's going on, but I love the atmosphere. My entire blended family is here in one room, laughing and cheering, sighing and shouting 'ooooh' and 'noooo' as if their lives depended on it, and all the other sound effects that go with football. The half-standing, half-seated 'chair position' when the team looks like they are about to score but then don't, is hilarious. I sit with Doug on my lap, participating in this magical event without having the faintest idea what's happening in footballing terms.

What I do see is a young man who has passion. Diego loves it.

Thankfully, Liverpool win the match.

After the game, Diego talks about his dad, about what a good footballer he was, and that they used to play football together when he was younger.

'Baby Tomas was too little to play, but Dad used to joke that he was growing his own team,' Diego says, as he talks about his other brothers joining in. They were all seriously into football, it seems. Most evenings, if the weather was not too bad, his dad would take him and his brothers to the park to play football.

None of this was in his referral. I'm guessing that was so he could not be identified, and he probably shouldn't be talking about it. But he's excited by the match he just watched. Lily sits quietly watching, taking it all in.

'But, I just wanted to say thanks for being brave enough to invite me into your home. Not everyone would do that, and I just want you to know that I'm *really* grateful.'

I tell him what good manners he has. He explains that good manners and politeness meant a lot to his parents, who had both been raised very strictly back in Portugal.

He talks about how much love there was in their home before things went bad and his dad left. How his father was always there. He made their home beautiful. He loved their little garden where he grew tomatoes and herbs for Diego's mum to use in her cooking.

I wonder if Diego should see his family. He must miss his mum and his brothers. Most foster children would have contact visits with their birth family, but perhaps it is too dangerous given Diego's particular situation. There must be a safe way that he can have contact with her online, though, even if they can't meet in person.

In the absence of a social worker, the only person I can contact is Simon. I guess he is acting in the role of Diego's social worker. I haven't seen a name for a social worker in any of the documentation, another peculiarity to this placement. But the more I think about it, the more I think I need to do some digging here and see if Diego can find a way to see his family. It must be months and months since he has seen them now, and that's hard.

Without a phone, he can't even message or speak to them.

Diego is still cheering at bedtime and the mood in the household is buoyant. This young man has certainly made an impact on our lives in a very short space of time.

VII

As the weeks go on, Lloyd and I help Diego turn his room into a passing approximation of a Liverpool Football Club gift shop.

My boys were never into sport to this extent. I'm finding the whole thing rather addictive. Every time I see something connected to Liverpool, I buy it.

I had a friend once, a long time ago, who warned about never telling people that you collect something. She herself collected frogs, or representations of them. She had three little frog statues in her loo, which rather gave the game away.

After a few years of everyone she knew buying her frog-related artefacts for every birthday and Christmas present, she begged people to stop. She was running out of room and was beginning to feel like the frog-equivalent of the crazy cat lady down the road.

I think I will have to stop soon, or Diego won't be able to move in his room.

We continue to chat daily to Ross, or Ben, or both; they

are usually together. I tell them about Diego's observations at school.

'He told me that kids are selling vapes in the toilets and playground, and that this is a sort of test, but that the teachers at school are in denial. He also says that when he walks around town he can see county lines everywhere. He thinks that things will only get worse.'

Ross and Ben are sympathetic to my 'revelations', but totally unsurprised. I'm not telling them anything they don't already know.

'But you should still inform the headteacher,' Ben advises.

'Diego also said that when he walked around with Jackson and Vincent after football down the park, they saw drug deals going on in broad daylight outside the Guildhall and no one batted an eyelid.'

The way county lines seems to have infiltrated the community in plain sight is truly shocking. Diego has walked around pointing out the suspicious barbers and nail bars to Jackson, who confirmed that they had only just arrived in town. Most town high streets are either rows of empty shopfronts, or else full of charity shops and cafés, alongside vape shops and barber shops that seem empty most of the time and must be a front for something else.

'The councils turn a blind eye to it, because they want the council tax, and these guys can pay it, it's nothing to them,' Ben explains. 'The economics works with county lines and it's all directly linked to the dark crime rings. You know how all humans stem from Africa? Well, most organised crime stems from the "Ndrangheta".'

'Really? I didn't know that.'

I have never heard of this before and have no idea what Ben is talking about. I get him to spell it. He explains that the 'Ndrangheta is a mafia-type criminal syndicate that has been going for a couple of hundred years and has developed into one of the world's most powerful and widespread organised crime entities.

And until recently, I had thought county lines was a newish thing.

'Old as the hills,' Ben says. 'And really clever. They use racism in each country to divide and rule, like in your town, Louise. I bet the police and the locals all think county lines is about trainlines, or only involves black men in beamers and 4x4s.'

'To be fair, Ben, you and Ross are both black men who drive a huge, black 4x4 and look like you'd be on the casting couch for a new drama about drug dealers.'

He laughs at that.

'Yeah, and that too.'

He went on to tell me that in the more rural areas it's white kids. Not just at the bottom. The elders and leaders are white.

'That's what's happening with all this racism shit that's going on right now around the country. In England it's used as a smoke screen. They're whipping people up, targeting hotels full of brown people, forgetting that the Albanian, Bulgarian and Russian mafia gangs are white. By getting everyone to hate black and brown faces, they allow that lot to carry on their business totally uninterrupted, because the police are all busy dealing with the racist shit.'

I have not thought of it like that before, as a distraction technique.

'Do you think all these people are in it together?'

Ben laughs. 'What do you think?'

As I talk to Ben, my head feels as if it's starting to spin. The more I learn, the scarier the world seems to be.

I can't do much against a tide of gangs and hate, but I can, at least, do as Ben suggested and contact the headteacher about some of the things that are going on. Not one for relying on one individual to do anything, I decide to contact the entire senior leadership team. I don't hold out a huge amount of hope for a bunch of busy teachers who seem too out of touch to understand this underworld. The ones with the most power seem to be bearded, middle-class and white, with lives so far removed from gang culture. And what can they do anyway? We can try.

Though even the act of reporting it becomes tricky. I

don't want to dob Diego in, so I need to be careful about my wording.

I would like to report that it has come to my attention…

I start typing, but realise immediately that putting it this way just sounds like gossip. You very quickly see how reporting county lines activity is virtually impossible. They will want evidence in order to do anything, and how do you provide evidence? These criminal gangs are good at what they do. I don't want to say 'clever' as Ben did. It's just levels of bullying, and I would also say that they are patient. They have waited for the perfect storm: smartphones, Brexit, Andrew Tate. It adds up to disaffected young men. A recent university study found that teenage boys will encounter misogynistic content online in a little over 20 minutes. If they click on anything, or respond in any way, their feed will be flooded with similar content. It's an onslaught. And there is no healthy blueprint for masculinity to counter it.

And to make things much worse, we're in a climate where the school system is totally geared up and focused on examination results, rather than actual education. It's all about academia, when only a small percentage of the population is properly 'academic'. It's easy to see how much our society's young men struggle in the midst of this toxic mix – where patriarchal notions are at least partially responsible for the tragically high male suicide rates. Boys really are sold a lie that makes them deeply miserable. How many young men walk around with their headphones on, hoods up, alone? What have we done to our children? It is very hard to be male in the current climate, let alone a male with Diego's history. I know he is putting a brave face on everything, but I wonder how sustainable that is in the long term, how he is really feeling beneath it all, and what's truly going on for him.

Which reminds me, I haven't done anything yet about contact visits. I message Simon.

Can Diego see his mum, his brothers? Is that possible?

Simon gets back to me quite quickly. It's a one-word answer: *Yes*.

Well, wow.

I didn't think it would be that straightforward. I am so pleased. I won't say anything to Diego until we have the details. But I tell Lloyd, and he is made-up for him. He, like me, was deeply moved when Diego talked about his dad and football. We need to learn more about what happened and see if we can try to understand.

Diego's very cheerfulness – that is so winsome – has also begun to worry me; the more I try to understand what has happened to him, the more I realise that this young man has been through so much – too much.

Kids who are pulled into county lines are criminalised by society for something that they had no choice about.

That alone will be very destructive, aside from the brutal crime he was forced to witness.

He smiles all the time, but I wonder if that smile is masking serious emotional hurt.

I'm reminded of that TV advert about men's mental health, where two football supporters went to every match together, sitting side by side, game after game. The audience are led to think that one is depressed – but it turns out to be his friend who committed suicide. It was brilliant and, because of the twist, got its message across in such a powerful way. But when I think about it, I worry about what's going on beneath the surface for Diego. He loves his mum, that's plain to see. And circumstances are keeping them apart. As far as I can work out, his family was a loving family that was dismantled by forces beyond their control. This boy, because that is what he is, just a boy, needs to see his mum.

I'm glad that Simon is onside.

The rest of the week passes. On Saturday, the boys play football down the park once more. It has already become routine. But today something is different. Vincent sends me a text.

Two men are standing around watching us. I think they're watching Diego.

Vincent and Jackson don't know the full story about Diego, but they know to be vigilant. The constant surveillance alerts have put us all on edge. We are all hypervigilant. I've told them all that if there is even the tiniest thing that seems out of the ordinary, however seemingly insignificant, they have to let us know. If something is worrying Vincent, then it should worry me too.

Lloyd is out and isn't answering his phone. There is a note on the kitchen table.

Just gone to B&Q to get drill bit.

I shut the backdoor and lock it, then pen another note of my own.

At park with boys, call me asap.

I should probably call Simon, but I can get there far more quickly than he can.

I think I knew, the moment we said Diego should come to us, that we would end up protecting him from dubious characters. I have a horrible feeling in the pit of my stomach. I realise that it's fear.

Here we go.

VIII

I drive to the road nearest the park, lock the car and march over to where I know the boys are. I'm ready to do battle with anyone who dares to touch one hair on any of my boys' heads. The fear has released a surge of adrenaline and I'll take anyone on.

Vincent looks at me, then nods in the direction of the two men. They don't look 'obviously' county lines, but then, as Ben, Ross and Simon have repeatedly explained, the profile of involvement isn't the stereotype we think it is. And you can't be too careful. One of them I think I have seen before. He has a little dog with him that I recognise.

I head straight over to them.

They smile, unconcerned.

I don't bother with niceties. 'Why are you interested in these boys?' I hear a strange sort of plumminess in my own voice. I sound a bit like Mrs Thatcher in her heyday. I don't know why it is, but when I'm really cross I sound posh – when every part of me in that moment is kicking about in the gutter.

The man without the dog says, 'I'm Dave and this is John. He's a local and he used to be a football scout back in the day. He gave me a call and said that there's this lad down the park kicking about with his mates and he's doing some moves that would blow my mind. He wasn't wrong.'

I frown. I'm caught off-guard. This is the last thing I expected. And I'm so paranoid, it could be a trap. 'Sorry, what? Who did you say you were?'

'Dave. Dave Thomas. Here's my card. Is he your lad?'

'He's living with us,' I say.

Dave folds his arms. 'Watch.'

I believe I have already mentioned the limitations of my football knowledge, i.e. I know next to nothing about it, but I do as I'm asked and watch them play.

Dave offers a running commentary. 'He's got speed, stamina, balance, the full monty. Look at that ball control. There. Did you see how he's passing to the young fella? Christ! Look at that shot into the goal. I've been watching him, he's got real composure on the ball. Look at that confidence. I know he's only in the park, but that makes it even more remarkable.'

The players who are losing are my sons, but I can take that.

'If he has the mental strength to go with it, then who knows?'

My phone rings.

It's Lloyd. 'Everything alright?'

'Yes. Vincent called to tell me that a couple of men were hanging around in the park watching Diego.'

Lloyd says, 'I'm coming now.'

'No, it's okay. I thought that too, but they're not county lines, they're football scouts.'

I notice Dave wince when I say 'county lines'.

'A football scout? I'm coming now,' Lloyd repeats.

We discover that we are living with some serious talent.

Diego is a 'natural' and Dave assures us that he will be a sought-after football player. We spend some time chatting. Diego explains that he's new to the area and has only just started at a new school, but is hoping to make the team. Dave promises to come and watch.

'Can you imagine the excitement in Liverpool if he goes on to play for Liverpool FC?' I say when we get home. I'm not sure I've ever said the words 'FC' out loud before, but they're on every bit of merch in Diego's room and I feel it adds a convincing air of authority to my football chat.

'Louise, that's not *exactly* how this works–'

I have absolutely no idea how it works, but I know that Diego must be feeling proud and excited. Although there will be more than a bit of pressure to go with it. I'm absolutely buzzing and I'm not even his mum. How will his mum feel when she finds out?

'But you heard him. He's going to be sought-after!'

Lloyd is a little bit more pragmatic. 'It's a bloke in the park who thinks Diego's got some talent. He hasn't signed a contract. Calm down. I'm afraid the Kop End aren't going to be cheering him on just yet.'

I don't know what that means, but it's miserable of Lloyd to rain on this parade.

I speak to Ben as soon as the coffee is on. He puts the phone on speaker; Ross is there. I'm starting to think they might be joined at the hip.

With great excitement I tell them how a football scout came to the park this morning and now he wants to see how Diego plays in a match. 'Isn't it brilliant? He said that he has so much talent!'

I hear one of them sigh, then Ross speaks. 'Oh, Louise. I am so sorry, but Diego cannot meet this scout. We have to close this down right now. He can't go to the park anymore.'

'What? He loves going to the park–'

'I know it's hard, but if those people get a whiff of his whereabouts Diego's life will be in danger.'

I feel myself sliding down a tube of disappointment.

'And yours,' Ben adds.

I feel so bad for Diego. How can life be so cruel?

'So, what then? He can't reveal his ability because of those fuckwits?'

Ross says, 'That's about the long and the short of it.'

'Look, we know it's shit,' Ben says. 'And, trust us, we have seen those skills.'

'He's certainly megged you a few times, mate,' Ross chuckles.

'But anything like this will attract attention, and that we can't afford.'

I am devastated. Today has been an emotional rollercoaster and we haven't even reached lunchtime. But if it's devastating for me, how much more so for Diego?

'Well, I don't know how to break that to him. Can you talk to him?'

'Where is he now?'

'Upstairs, gaming with Vincent.'

We've checked this out and it's allowed. Diego has a new online name so no one will know it's him, and Ben and Ross can monitor it remotely.

Ben says, 'We'll be at yours in an hour.'

Lloyd has not stopped smiling, however much he might want to pretend to downplay the encounter with the scout. He is as excited as I am for Diego and all the possibilities it presents for his future.

But now it's my turn to rain on *his* parade and tell him the news.

At first he's incredulous, and then he's just sad, very sad, that this talented, lovely young man cannot have the opportunities he should have because of the drug dealers.

'It's more than petty drug-dealing, Lloyd,' I remind him. 'It's big crime. It's the dark crime rings that he has seen the faces of.'

I wonder whose faces they are.

I try very hard not to think of *Scooby Doo* and how, at the end of the show, they pull the masks off the ghosts and monsters who have been terrorising the hotel and reveal that, actually, it was the owner all along. On second thoughts, perhaps *Scooby Doo* should come back and do a modern version, based on county lines. Or a whole series. After all, county lines is only one aspect, one branch of the dark, international crime rings. The ones sitting at the top probably have friends in very high places.

Poor Diego.

Ross and Ben arrive within the hour, as promised. There's no mistaking it because Lloyd's phone pings with alerts, and this time it isn't the ginger thug-cat, nor is it me walking across the garden to bring the washing in.

I meet them outside and, before we go into the house, I check that it's still okay for Diego to be in touch with his mum.

'Absolutely. We'll talk to you about how we're going to manage that,' Ross promises.

I call Diego down. As he makes his way down the

stairs, the scent of Versace's 'The Dreamer for Him' wafts with him. The Eau de Toilette was his choice and far more bearable than the ubiquitous Lynx Africa, although I've had to explain to him that he shouldn't leave it out on the windowsill in the sun or the smell will go. He is very pleased with his bottle of 'manhood' and has since been careful to position it – still on display in his room – but on the side in the shade.

They all greet each other with knuckles and elbows. I think it's sweet and, at the same time, slightly over the top. Then again, I'm a middle-aged woman who does not do this sort of thing.

'I'm tempted to start doing that,' I say.

It's a joke, of course, but the look Diego gives me confirms that, whatever happens, I definitely should *not* start doing it.

They sit down together at the kitchen table. I turn down the roast in the oven, not knowing how long this will take. Ross and Ben both comment on how nice it smells. I bet they've been living off McDonald's.

Before they deliver the bad news, I get in first with something cheerier.

'So, any news on Diego being able to chat to his mum?'

Diego lights up.

I'm pleased. This way, the bad news will not feel quite so bad, diluted by some good.

I must teach Ross and Ben about difficult conversations. They are an art form in their own right.

'Diego can talk to his mum later today. She said at 6pm?'

That is perfect. Not too far away and not so close that he has no time to prepare. Just enough time to let it all sink in. They explain that he must not say where he is, nor must I appear on camera.

'But you have to stay in the room. If Diego looks like he will say something, or worse, does actually say something that could give his whereabouts away, then you need to close down the lid on the laptop and call us immediately.'

They tell Diego that his mum has also been briefed and that a worker will be sitting beside her, off-camera, with the same instructions.

'Today you have 15 minutes. Anything longer than that starts to become a risk. Louise, can you ensure that there are no images or clues on the wall or in frame that could give your location away?'

This is, of course, all doable and Lloyd comes in to hear all the instructions, too, so I don't have to explain it again.

Ross leans forward and puts both hands on the table. 'Now, Diego, you are not going to like what I say next.'

Diego interrupts. 'I know. You don't have to say it. I can't do football anymore.'

He's worked it out for himself. I look at his face. He is putting the brave one on, pretending to be okay. This is how Diego operates.

I resist saying anything, as I know that I can't promise a thing.

I sit down, then decide that in itself is a mistake. I am imposing myself into the conversation and I shouldn't. I stand back up and go and move a few things around on the side, looking busy. Carrots, I'll do the carrots. I chop them into slices because it's easier than batons, they always seem to go wonky when I do them.

Ross and Ben stay for an hour, so of course, I offer them dinner. I know these two would love nothing more than a Sunday roast feast, especially Ross who is intermittently distracted by the smells all the way through the meeting, but they decline politely.

'We'll hit Burger King on the way to the motorway,' Ben says, looking reluctantly in the direction of the oven.

When I've shown them out, I go back into the kitchen. It's quiet now, just Diego left.

He stands up. I walk up to him and say, 'Come here.'

I open my arms and he walks in for a hug. I put my arms around him and squeeze. His body begins to shake. And then he cries and cries and cries.

Lloyd walks back in. I look at him over Diego's shoulder. Perhaps he should leave. I'm not sure that Diego would want to be seen crying in front of another man. But Lloyd walks up to us and puts his hand on Diego's back.

'It will be alright, Diego,' he says, very gently. 'Your day will come.'

We all stand in this huddle for as long as it takes for Diego to stop feeling the need to be here, nestled in this warmth and care.

My legs are hurting by the time he breaks away.

IX

Even Jackson eats some of the roast, without six eggs as extra gym-fuel, and Lily manages to sit at the table without staring and flirting (perhaps the novelty of Diego is beginning to wear off).

Once they have all dispersed and I'm clearing everything up, I ask Lloyd to visit each of the children and tell them not to come into my office at 6pm. And to explain why.

'Also, can you explain to them that football is off the cards until we find somewhere where Diego's skills aren't going to be noticed.'

I can't think of an answer about where that will be, as yet. Perhaps on the moon. You cannot *not* notice Diego's talent, it seems.

The dishwasher goes on and I leave Doug enjoying a few leftovers in his bowl, balanced by the dog food he should be eating. I head to the studio and make sure it's a suitable space for Diego to talk to his mum in. I move an easel bearing my current project out of the way, in case my style is distinctive enough to be recognised. Ross will send over a link from a made-up email account five minutes before the meeting. I am to submit a code to enter the video meeting that he will send me via WhatsApp.

I look at my watch. It's 5.30pm. I go and see Diego and, bless his heart, he has had a shower, done his hair and sprayed himself with The Dreamer. How appropriate that fragrance now seems. He has even tidied up his bedroom, though it still looks like a Liverpool Football Club shrine. He's not bad at housework, which, in a teenage boy, is usually a good indication that they've spent time as a carer.

'I don't think there will be time to show your mum your room today, but maybe next time you can talk to her from in here and show it to her – and let her see her how tidy it is.'

Diego tells me that in their old house he shared a very small room with Andre. 'Mama has the big room. We talked about swapping round because it could fit three of us in easily, but she liked keeping it as it was, in case Daddy came home.'

I look up at the word 'Daddy'. It seems incongruous coming from the mouth of a strapping teenager. What a sweetheart he is. It's been a long, long time since I've heard Vincent or Jackson call Lloyd, 'Daddy'. He sees me looking.

'Sounds stupid now, I know. But that's what we called

him. Not Papa. He wanted it English. Everything English.' There's a hint of bitterness that has crept into his tone. He doesn't usually let that through, though he must feel it. I sit down on the chair – though I have to move some sportswear to do so.

'Are you okay, Diego?'

He looks at me, a bit puzzled.

'Are you excited about seeing your mum?'

He shrugs. 'It's been a long time.'

There is a pause. I wait for as long as I dare, to allow him to fill it.

'When I last saw her, she was not in a good way.'

Another pause.

'My mum drinks. She started when Daddy left us.'

I *sort of* knew that, but not much was in the referral, for obvious reasons. I don't want to ask too much more, because I have been told that there are things we really should not know, for his safety and ours. Loose tongues cost lives, and all that.

But I am looking at a beautiful young boy who has been through so much distress in his short life. For goodness sake, he witnessed a murder.

He is not allowed any help, it seems, or even to do the one thing that brings him joy: football – because he is too good at it. It is so bloody unfair. There's no justice, sometimes.

I stand up and look out of the window.

Fuck it!

'Diego, after you talk to your mum, let's turn the lawn into a football pitch.'

There is a flicker of animation.

'Yes. We can all move the pots and furniture and, to be honest with you, Diego, the bloody lawn will grow back. It's only grass. Let's get you practising!'

He stands up too, and smiles. 'Louise, you are a lovely mama.'

I hold back the tears and also know that Vincent and Jackson will have a bit of a view on this new development, after years of me telling them not to rag up the lawn.

I look at my watch again. The minutes are ticking by. 'Right, come on. Let's do this.'

He follows me down to my studio that has now been transformed into a neutral office – which happens when I have to do proper grown-up stuff.

I have cleared the sketchbooks and paints and brushes off my table. I have prepared everything in the studio, or at least as far as I can. All that will appear behind Diego on screen is one corner of one of my abstract paintings. I'm not sure gangs are interested in art. Actually, I do remember Simon saying that they *are*, but not through appreciation, only financial value; so they definitely won't be interested in mine.

He sits down. I move my chair to the side, away from the camera, so that I can see the screen at an angle but I'm not in shot. This feels intrusive but we have no choice. The text comes through as arranged. I turn the laptop around towards me, click on the link and tap in the code, away from Diego. I turn the laptop back around and sit down. We wait.

After a moment, Diego says, 'There's nothing there.'

I turn the laptop back to me and see that I have to click on another link. I hear a female voice – so I quickly turn it back to Diego. His mum does not want to see me! I put my head down and look at my hands.

'Ai, meu filho!'

My Portuguese is extremely limited, but I guess that must be 'my boy' or 'my son'.

'Como estás?'

I think that's 'How are you?'

Then I hear a man's voice in the background. 'In English, please.'

She says, 'Okay.'

I look up at Diego. His eyes are full of tears. For all his tough talk, he is letting a great deal out today. Perhaps the floodgates have opened.

'Mama, how are you?'

At first, the conversation is a bit awkward – stilted and very slow. Of course it is. It is months since they have seen each other. Diego can't have seen her since before he went missing after the murder. Doing it through a screen doesn't help. The glass is a barrier and sometimes there is a slight delay, so they speak over the top of each other and then stop, waiting for the other.

Gradually, through the tears that both shed, come genuine words from a mother to her son and a son to his mother.

She keeps saying that she is sorry, she is so sorry. That if she had not been drinking, he would not have gone to the foodbank. Maria, I'm guessing an auntie? Or a friend or neighbour, worked out that the foodbank was being watched by criminals. Maria ran up to the car, bashed on the window and called them murderers. This was filmed by a passer-by which was good because he captured the number plate. The foodbank now has CCTV facing all directions to protect children and other users of their service.

Wow. I don't know who this Maria is, but I like the sound of her.

Diego asks how his brothers are.

'They are good. They miss you. Maria is over with me most days, and her husband, too. They help out with the boys. Andre is very good. He is just like you.'

Diego's mum sounds lovely. Soft and kind. But she is clearly in a great deal of emotional pain. Her voice cracks at times, or drops to a plaintive whisper.

Diego talks about the food. He tells his mum that I have cooked bacalhau for him.

In any other circumstances, she would probably want to give me her recipe. I hear sounds in the background and also notice that there are only five minutes left of the allotted 15.

'Can I see my brothers?' Diego looks at me for an answer.

They are outside in the hall, waiting.

I quickly text Ross and he messages straight back. *Yes.*

I can tell that the worker at the other end has also been given the nod. Three mini versions of Diego come flying into the lounge and stand behind his mum.

The man at the other end speaks sternly. 'No one must say his name, is that absolutely clear? His name for now is Diego. You must not say his name!'

The room quietens and my heart sinks. There are nicer ways of saying these things. Then, one of the younger ones puts his hand on the screen.

Diego does the same.

The others join in. Touching hands across the miles.

Diego tells Andre that it's his turn to step up and be the man of the house.

Then the 15 minutes are up.

Diego's mum whispers, 'I love you.' Tears are falling down her face and I realise that they are falling down mine, too.

I wipe them away and click the button to 'leave meeting'.

Diego hangs his head and breaks down.

I move my chair close to his and hold him.

'I want my mama,' he sobs.

X

Sunday evening's sadness settles over the whole household. It's in the air, palpable, and I don't know how to lift it.

I sit on the sofa while Lloyd tries to find a new series for us to watch on Netflix. Sometimes, by the time a decision has been made, it has taken longer than an episode of watching something.

Diego has gone to his room and I have let him. I think it's best to give him some space.

Jackson comes downstairs and into the sitting room.

'Mum, is Diego okay? I heard crying from his room.'

'Yes, sweetheart, he will be. I think it's just very hard for him because he hasn't seen them for months.'

Jackson looks so sad for his foster brother.

Vincent comes in a moment later and asks the same question. Jackson explains it to Vincent, who also looks sad. It's a lot to take in. Then comes Lily, holding a picture she has made for Diego.

'Can I see?'

It's a card with a football, but in each of the white

hexagons on the ball there are little messages of hope: quotations and epigrams.

'As the only one here who is separated from their family, I think I understand him the most,' she says.

'Lily, that is true and thoughtful. But it doesn't tell the whole truth. I also grew up in foster care and have been separated from my family all my life.'

She knows this, of course.

'And you are all my family. Lily, we *are* your family. Family doesn't have to be one particular thing. It can mean many things. It's more about the people in your life right now. The people who help you, who love you and who support you. You may move on from us, but you will always have experienced "family", whatever that means.'

Again, it's a discussion we've had before.

'And Lily, you also know that there are plenty of children you have met while being in our family whose birth families were toxic and dangerous. So, can I ask you to think on this, please?'

Lloyd throws me a look, and Vincent and Jackson stand waiting for Lily's reply, with an attitude that says, 'Don't mess with the lioness!'

They are right because, right now, I feel the pain that Diego's mum feels. No, that's a lie. I can never feel the depth of pain that she is experiencing, of course I can't. But I am certainly feeling something, and it's about being a mother and the pain of loss. I know only too well that not all mothers are good. The very nature of my work shows me over and over again that many are not. But I heard something in Diego's mother's voice that has affected me. There was love and pain. Equally hard to see was the joy of his little band of brothers when they saw Diego, quickly followed by their sadness at not being able to reach out to him, and the punch of not being able to call him by his name.

Lily leaves the room.

In this moment, I honestly don't care if she is sulking or in a huff. Sometimes plain-speaking is the only thing that will do. Despite being in care, Lily has so much privilege and love, so I can't be apologetic.

She comes back a few moments later with a pen. 'Would you all like to sign the card?'

That's better!

When the children disperse, I pop upstairs to see Diego.

'Hi, how are you doing? Are you okay?'

His eyes are red and wet when he looks up at me. He tries to wipe a tear away, as if he's furious with himself.

'Would you like to come downstairs and watch TV with me and Lloyd?'

He shrugs, but it's not a no. He doesn't need to be on his own any longer. I hold out my arm to encourage him.

He stands up. I pull him in for another hug and he rests his head silently on my shoulder.

After a few seconds, I push him back and look into his face. 'Bloody gorgeous boy! Your mum must be so proud of you.'

We walk downstairs. I ask if he'd like a hot chocolate and a sandwich.

'Yes, please.'

I don't blame him. I think that much emotion would make anyone hungry. He hovers next to me while I assemble a ham, cheese, lettuce and pickle sandwich. I put a bag of crisps on the side of the plate for good measure. I hand him the plate and we return to the sitting room. I carry the hot chocolate in for him and then settle down in my little spot, next to the sidelight and table. He sits near me. I hand him the card that now has messages from all of us. He reads it and smiles.

Lloyd is *still* flicking through Netflix, so quickly now that I can't see what he's looking at.

'Lloyd, slow down,' I say.

Then he says, 'There's nothing here.'

'It's not just about you,' I reply, with a smile, although my inner voice is saying something far ruder. Sometimes too much choice is a big problem.

Diego eats his sandwich, drinks his hot chocolate and moves his chair around so that he is sitting close to me. He is clearly craving affection, because he leans his head on my shoulder once more. I put my arm around him. Lloyd moves up and sits close to him on the other side. This is our way of saying, 'We've got you, Diego.'

We watch something in the end, but I couldn't tell you what it was. I have no memory of it. I'm too swept up in my own thoughts, and feeling so many emotions for and with Diego.

It's not a Sunday I want to re-live.

On Monday, after school, we all help to move the garden around so that all my pots (and there are many) are well away from the lawn. The garden furniture is moved down to the far end. I take a good look at all my flowers and plants and apologise to them. We set up goal posts at either end, roughly hewn from old bits of wood that we found in the loft. It's not quite Wembley Stadium, but it's plenty big enough for Diego to move about and keep up his practice.

The boys don't say a word about the fact that I've never allowed them to do this, only, 'Is this alright, Diego?'

Diego stands in the garden with his hands on his hips, white Nike socks pulled up high, his feet in his sliders. He looks around and makes the best face, as if he's a town planner appraising a new building.

'That's boss, yeah, sound!'

We look at him and laugh. We have learnt that the

Liverpudlians – or this one, at least – have a wonderful way of being understated about things that are really good.

'Fancy a game, lads?'

I'm not sure if Diego means just the boys by 'lads'. Lloyd, Lily and me are all standing on the new football pitch.

Lily is definitely including herself. 'Can I be goalie?'

'I'll be ref!' Lloyd says.

'And I'll be indoors,' I say firmly.

Through the kitchen window I watch Diego put his trainers on. Vincent and Jackson are ready and Lily is doing a strange dance in the goal. I hope she doesn't lean on it. I'm not sure about its sturdiness.

I'm proud of my little family and this community of kindness and friendship. I also love the endless inventiveness in sport. This new game of football is all about trying to stop Diego getting from one end of the pitch to the other. The gladiators, Jackson and Vincent, never manage to prevent him. It's almost comedic the way Diego dances around them each time. Even with my pathetic knowledge, I know the scouts in the park were absolutely right. I have never seen anyone so natural at anything.

While they continue to charge about and Lily does her funny little dances at one end, and Lloyd keeps bending over, with one arm in the air, breathing very heavily as he tries to keep up with the pace, I make lots of sandwiches and snacks. They'll all be hungry after so much running around.

Lloyd's phone is on the kitchen table, pinging like crazy with all the movement around the house. Those cameras must be worn out. I might lose my flowers but, on the upside, all the activity will keep that vile ginger tom out of our garden. The light is beginning to go. It will soon be time to turn the clocks back. But it doesn't seem to stop them. Perhaps we need to invest in some floodlights. God help us!

XI

By all accounts, Diego seems to be doing pretty well at school. He's a bright lad and obviously excels at sport, and also in languages. He's doing Spanish GCSE (because Portuguese isn't available) and says that although the pronunciation is different, there are enough similarities in vocabulary, grammar and word order between Spanish and Portuguese, or so he tells me, to make it relatively easy and put him ahead of most of the class. He's also studying French, which doesn't come so naturally, but perhaps already being bilingual makes it easier to learn a third and fourth language.

Teachers seem to like him because he's polite, but also has the confident banter that never goes too far. The air of maturity must appeal to them, as it does to us.

The female students like him because he's good-looking in that swarthy, Mediterranean way, and the Liverpudlian accent makes him cool and different, an exotic species. The fan club, started by Lily, seems to be collecting more members by the day, which must give him ever more kudos. The boys like him because he's so very good at football.

He says he was bullied at his old school, but here his Liverpool background gives him a kind of street-cred. Because he doesn't give too much away about himself, he no doubt comes across as quite mysterious, which can have its own appeal, too.

Moreover, because of his past, he knows exactly who is safe to be around and who is not. And he reckons there are certainly some characters to stay away from. Vincent nods at the names he mentions as being slightly dodgy.

He reports more sightings of county lines activity at school. I keep emailing the school's senior leadership team with each update, but they don't even reply.

An acknowledgement would be nice. I consider it bloody rude that they just get ignored.

I have no evidence, of course, just Diego's observations, but it would be nice to know that I'm not just emailing into a void.

When we are out and about, just walking to the shops or going out on a dog-walk, he is like an alley cat. He is hyper-vigilant and moves in a way that is cautious, low-to-the-ground. It's the movement a fox or feral cat might make to avoid humans. But it's not submissive. He manages to appear independent and streetwise at the same time.

But it must be exhausting being this alert the whole time.

On Friday night, he comes with me to the chip shop to pick up our takeaway order. We arrive a few minutes before it's due to be collected and, from where we are parked, we can see the whole street: the pubs, restaurants, everything. We sit back in the car, like Starsky and Hutch on a stakeout.

'Look right,' he instructs.

I do, but see nothing.

'Wait, watch.'

A grey, newish BMW slows down by the entrance to an alley. The alley is gated. A man in a hoodie comes through the gate and takes something from the car. The car drives off and the man goes straight back through the gates and locks them.

'Was that a drug delivery?' I ask.

Diego nods. 'Look to the left, next to the pub.'

I do, and see three boys, aged about 11 or 12, appear. They are on electric scooters and zoom up towards the pub. A few men, who I'd say from this distance are probably in their 50s and 60s, come out of the pub. They look like working men, builders, perhaps.

'They love a bit of lemon, that lot,' Diego says. 'They get tanked up, do coke to straighten themselves out, then go home and beat their wives and torture their dogs.'

They look so very ordinary. If you'd asked me to pick out the drug-takers from this scene, I wouldn't have picked them. I make a sighing sound. If this is happening on my doorstep, it must be happening in every town and village in the country.

'Look at the gate again.'

'What's happening now?'

'Does that alleyway go to the back of the shops and flats in the next street?' Diego asks.

I nod. 'Yes, it does. Why?'

'Watch.'

Five kids, two on scooters, come through the gate. They disperse up and down the street. They are all in the uniform of black hoodies beneath puffer jackets with cross-body bags on top.

'They're the soldiers,' Diego says.

'Do you know them?' I ask. 'Are they at your school?'

'Yeah, they're all at my school and the teachers don't give a fuck.'

I don't pick him up on the language. I guess it comes with the territory. But I do feel angry about what's going on, right under everyone's noses. Why isn't it just stopped? I want to do something about it, but I know we can't do anything right now.

'Come on. Let's go and get dinner.'

We stand in the chip shop and, while we're waiting, we

both turn to face the street. Diego in his shorts and grey hoodie, with the long socks and sliders. He has his arms folded. He catches my eye and tilts his head to indicate that I should look again. More deals. It's everywhere. It's insane. I'm never going to be able to look at this place in the same way again. Once you see it, it appears obvious.

When our order is ready, we take the thin white plastic bag, full up with warm paper parcels, and head back to the car. Diego holds the bag on his lap and the aroma soon fills the car. I love the smell of fish and chips, especially trapped like this in a small space where the smells have nowhere else to go. I can almost taste it. My mouth begins to water.

We drive past the kebab shop.

'Slow down,' Diego says.

I do. We both look in through the glass-front of the kebab shop. There are two men behind the counter, one clocks us immediately. We can hardly look like a threat, though. A middle-aged woman driving a teenager. There are a load of kids, boys and girls aged between 12 and 16 at a guess, hanging about in and just outside the shop.

'The man who owns the shop drives a brand new Bentley Bentayga and his wife drives a top of the range BMW i8.'

'That's nice.'

Diego looks across at me. 'Right. And how do you get to drive vehicles like that from selling kebabs?'

We drive and turn left along the road.

'Do you want more?'

I'm not sure that I do. I'm already feeling depressed, but he asks me to slow down once more.

'On your left, that flat above the tattoo shop.'

I look and see nothing.

'Have a good look.'

I look up and see another alley to the side of the tattoo place. A few young lads are walking into a side door. It's grubby down the alley. It looks unloved.

'Go on, then. What's going on there?'

We're on the road which runs parallel to the fish and chip shop.

'The kids we saw on the other side, the soldiers, they shift the drugs and move them out the back through the alley. But that flat is where they cook them.'

That can't be right. I think I know the old man who lives there. He used to run an antique shop where the tattoo shop is now.

When I tell Diego, he shrugs. 'I bet he's still there. Or dead. Have you seen him lately?'

I shake my head. 'Not now you mention it.'

'I bet they've cuckooed him, then. That's what happens.'

In movies, I think. Not in my hometown.

But Diego is insistent. 'The gang I worked for used

nice ladies in the area to scout out where the vulnerable people lived. Someone with dementia, living alone, made a great target. Perfect. They'd make friends with 'em and then the gang would move in.'

I'm beginning to feel sick. 'Let's go home.'

I don't think I have felt this level of despair in a long time.

I've looked after girls who have been caught up in county lines. Marilyn was one. She was a pickle. We managed to get her out of the area. But I thought she was unusual. I had no idea, until recently, it was such a big operation, or that so many children were involved, all being exploited.

Despite my earlier appetite and the delicious smells in the car, I no longer feel so hungry. Later I ask Diego if Simon, Ross and Ben know all the stuff that he's shared with me this evening.

'Yeah, of course. It's everywhere, Louise. Not just here. It's just that down here, no one knows me, so the gangs here don't know who I am. And I need to keep it that way.'

'Do you feel safe, Diego?'

'Yeah, Louise, I think so. As long as I don't get involved. And I won't. I keep meself to meself at school, I avoid the older kids, I'm a nerd, a geek, I do chess club and Lego club at lunchtime to keep meself away from the corridors.' He laughs. 'That's what Simon does, he turns us all into fucking geeks.'

On Sunday afternoon, Diego is in the garden, teaching football skills to Lily and her friend, Ellie. It's quite funny to watch. I think Lily has calmed her crush down and now sees Diego as another brother. Ellie, on the other hand, still seems starstruck. It's a bit like watching a strange version of *The Benny Hill Show.* She keeps picking up the ball and running with it. Lily is actually getting quite cross with her. Diego is being patient and polite, but I don't think this will happen again, not with Ellie.

I sit at the kitchen table while Lloyd cooks dinner. I like being off-duty in that department, and Lloyd is a good cook. I actively encourage him and the boys to cook as much as possible. In Vincent and Jackson's case, particularly, I like to see it as one of my little acts of kindness to their future partners. What's not to like about a man who is at home in the kitchen? I hope their future partners will enjoy delicious, homecooked meals, as I do: good food without the hassle, only the clearing up. And I can verify that clearing up is much, much easier when I haven't had to do all the cooking as well.

Hopefully I will, one day, also be able to educate my men to use the bloody dishwasher as a dishwasher. But now is not the moment to grumble.

Lloyd is making, based on another image from our tea

towel of cocktail recipes, pina coladas, though without the blousy umbrellas and kitsch things on straws. If I was in a cocktail bar, I wouldn't say no to all the little embellishments and decorations, but Lloyd is much more tasteful than me. I don't mind. I'm happy having regular taste-failures. The cocktails put me in the party mood. I sit with my laptop open, browsing.

'Why don't we go away for a long weekend? We can time it with the October half-term break.'

I would love to go abroad. We haven't had a break for a long time and I know we are all in need of one, but, as always with foster children, it's not that simple. Sometimes they don't want to go at all because such a trip would be completely out of their comfort zone: more change and break from routine. Sometimes they want to go but, as was the case with Marilyn, her behaviour could be a risk. And, if we do take a foster child away, we have to fund it all.

This time, we can't take Diego out of the country. I'm sure *he* would be fine, but his name isn't even Diego, so there is no chance of a passport and documents. I rule that idea out immediately. Instead, I look at places available in Cornwall. For all of us to go, it's looking like a few grand.

It makes me a bit fed up, because that would pay for an all-inclusive week somewhere abroad, including flights.

After another pina colada, Lloyd says, 'Wales?'

It's a good idea. Wales wasn't on my radar. We haven't

been there as a family. I did go to the Brecon Beacons on a school trip, years ago. I remember it was stunning and that we had a complete laugh. Yes, Wales.

I search accommodation in Wales and up pop lots of lovely looking places. Not only that, they're half the price of the ones in Cornwall, which appears to have become London-by-the-sea – at least in terms of the price of accommodation.

Lily sends Ellie home before dinner and carries on playing with Diego, just the two of them. She is getting on well with him now and he is actually teaching her to pass the ball. There is less dancing and more *actual* football. The other boys are in their rooms doing their own thing.

I call them all down to eat, apart from Jackson, who shows no sign of budging from his egg diet – and, my word, has his bedroom become a no-go zone as a result.

Over dinner, I sound them out about a little holiday in South Wales. It's a hit. Diego is all over it, and shares that he stayed somewhere in North Wales, in a little remote village, while he was in the third or fourth different place in an effort to try to lose the gang. I hope that won't present a problem. I won't book anything: I need to check it all with Ross, Ben and Simon. I give Simon a call.

'Yes, Louise. I think so. Your family life shouldn't be jeopardised because Diego is staying, and Diego also needs to feel as normal as he can. But Ross and Ben will need to be close by, just in case. They can also set up temporary cameras before you arrive.'

Ah, the pinging that has become the soundtrack to our lives. It was too much to hope that we might escape *that* for a few days.

It also strikes me that this must all cost a fortune. But, I suppose, not as much as crime.

When I tell Jackson, he immediately asks what restaurants are nearby. I take that as an indication that he will have a few days break from his high-protein egg and gym diet.

I feel excited. Half term is but a week and a half away. Not only will we get away for a nice break, but we'll have some respite from the bastard ginger cat. A few clicks and it is done. Cymru dyma ni'n dod – or, look out, Wales, here come the Allens!

XII

I am feeling very pleased with myself. I have managed to find a house in Wales to sleep all six of us, for not a lot more than half the cost of staying in Cornwall – and not a pasty in sight.

It takes us nearly four hours to get there. We decide to make the journey in both cars, as a little convoy. More petrol, but the only comfortable way to fit us and all our stuff in. It's never been worth investing in a seven-seater because, even though we'd all fit as passengers, we still wouldn't have the room to put in everyone's bags. It's fine driving both cars occasionally. I don't mind. I pack extra snacks to keep everyone fuelled on the journey. And it's all worth it, because, when we arrive, it's perfect. Our accommodation is a beautiful stone building on a rugged coastline. It even has a little indoor pool, so if the weather is bad, we can still swim. Everyone is happy.

We are on the outskirts of a small town. Within walking distance are several restaurants and three different pubs. There is also a proper-looking chip shop. I decide that, as a first-night treat, we'll go to the chip shop. Lloyd has brought a selection of wine, beers and lagers with us. Jackson is old enough to have a can. Surprisingly, perhaps because we offer it, he declines – preferring water and a smoothie. Jackson has, apparently, packed his smoothie maker, but no eggs! Thank the lord for a break from that smell. And he will deign to join us for a fish and chip supper, which is big of him.

There are fields all around us and the boys are straight off to the nearest one with the ball. While Lily, Lloyd and I unpack, I message Ross and Ben to see where they are. They have also managed to book a place nearby; a little cottage at the end of the road. It's actually very reassuring to have them so close.

Would you like anything from the chip shop? I text. Almost before I've finished typing the message, they come back with a resounding yes.

We invite them over to our house to eat. We have seating for nine and it's about time we all sat down together. After all, collectively we are Diego's weird temporary family. They play football with the boys. I don't have to look out of the window, as I can watch them on camera, out in the field next to the house. They have already installed the temporary security cameras on our place and on their cottage.

I go to the chip shop and end up spending over £100.

What a hungry lot they are. Lloyd has already prepared the table and in I come with two large bags of goodies. We all sit down and relax. Ross and Ben have one beer each and that's it. Lloyd and I enjoy ourselves. After dinner, the men all go back outside to play football. Lloyd has gone from being ref to football manager. He stands on the side with his arms folded, making strange sounds. But he's having fun. They all are.

For the rest of the trip, Ross and Ben stay close by, but they don't join us in the same way. Perhaps they sense that we need this chill out time together as a family and don't want to intrude.

On Saturday morning, we head down to the beach. It's a little windy, but the sun is shining and we spend the whole day there, with a picnic lunch. It is magical. We have great fun teaching Diego the rudiments of beach cricket. I wonder, in the light of his football prowess, how he feels about not being the best at it immediately. Lloyd's phone pings occasionally to tell us that someone is near the house, but that's just the odd local walking a dog, or Ross and Ben keeping an eye.

It really is a magnificent few days: totally relaxing, a break from routine, lots of laughs and silliness. All the things that a holiday should be. The weather even stays fine for us. When it's time to go home, we are all sad to pack up and leave. Ross and Ben stay behind to take down the cameras after we have gone. They've made it really easy for us, and been very unobtrusive. It makes me realise how much is possible, even under difficult circumstances, with the right resources.

We have a good drive home, not too much traffic on the road and a straightforward journey. Because we got off straightaway on the first weekend, there are a good few days of half term still left to enjoy.

The first thing I do when we get back is go round to our neighbours to pick up Douglas. I have missed our little pooch. These particular neighbours are his favourite hosts. They tell me that Doug seemed depressed while we were away, and they think he must be missing Dotty. He's not the only one. I still miss her so much. She was a right little madam at times. But perhaps it's the ones with character and personality we miss the most, despite their propensity to be a pain. We think she had the equivalent of doggy-ADHD. She could be a bit hectic and she was also stubborn. If it rained, she ran and hid in her bed and pretended to be invisible so that I wouldn't take her on a walk. But the neighbours' words bother me a little.

I hate to think of Doug as lonely.

It's true that he has the cats for company, which isn't actually as weird as it might sound. He and Mabel are quite tight, probably because Lily appears to have raised her cat like a human. We think that Mabel might actually believe she's a dog. There is certainly no cat and dog antagonism between them. But, however doglike she is, she's not Dotty. Cats don't do what dogs do. They are dismissive and use us like slaves, whereas dogs, on the whole, want to be loved and want to please. I love dogs. I would have loads of them, a whole pack, probably, if I didn't have Lloyd as a husband. He *tolerates* the animals, but he wouldn't choose them. He didn't grow up with pets. I did, and feel strange when I haven't got one with me. Maybe it's time to begin thinking about another dog. Not for me, you understand, but as a companion for Doug.

We have planned that this Sunday evening, before they go back to school, Diego will talk to his mum and his little brothers again. I asked Simon if he can have more time, this time, and we have agreed two lots of 15 minutes with a five-minute break in the middle. It's to stop any tracking, apparently. Tech has changed everything, including crime. I have suggested that he spends the first half with mum, then brings in his excited little brothers for act two. The same safety protocols apply as last time round, and this time Diego's brothers have received some education and training on what they can and can't say in advance of the call. Last time I felt a little bit uncomfortable with the brusque way the worker spoke to the boys; they should have been better-prepared.

As the weeks have gone on, Diego has become more

open and increasingly willing to let us inside that tough exterior. He says, with his body language at least, when he needs support, and I have learned to read the signs. When he puts his head in his hands, that is a sign that he needs our attention and reassurance. Like many first-born children with younger siblings, I think he has suffered from a deficit of affection. Just like my boys, he loves a hug every now and then. He has become very attached to Lloyd, who will stand out in the garden with him, encouraging him and cheering him on, come rain or shine. I try not to look too hard at the devastation of my beautiful garden and the sacrifice made to football. It will grow back and, if it doesn't, then it wasn't meant to live. I like sprinkling seeds into the gaps. I always forget I've done it, like when I plant bulbs, and when they grow, I feel like I've won a prize.

Diego likes to hang behind after dinner when the others have zoomed off to their rooms to do what it is they do. He has started to open up about his family. He told me how he feels saddest for his youngest brother who never had the experience of being born into a happy family like the rest of them did. 'At least me, Andre and Dinas know what the good times were like, but not Tomas, he came into our world when it was all sadness and poverty. That's all he's ever known.'

It's an unexpectedly perceptive way for a teenager to think, and it shows me how much he thinks and feels about other people. So often he seems to put himself last on the list of people to think about.

He has also begun to open up more and more about the time he spent in the gang and his involvement in county lines. We've reached a stage of trust in our relationship where I feel like I can ask him questions without being too intrusive. We prefer these conversations not to happen in front of the others, to protect him and them. A few times we stay up very late into the night talking. There's something about the small hours of the morning that means you can say things that you might not say at other times of the day.

One night, Diego tells me how he was first recruited. 'It was at the foodbank. I didn't know that the elders–'

I have to interrupt often for little points of clarification. He tells me that the 'elders' are actually about 19 or 20 years old and have been involved since they were little kids.

'They watch out for kids like me. I hate thinking about that bit, that they were watching, for weeks, probably. It makes me feel sick.'

'So how were you first approached? What happened?'

'They must have seen me with the picture of Diogo.'

Ah, Diogo Jota, (I now know) the footballer.

'I loved that man. He was like a god. He wasn't just a brilliant footballer, it was everything about him. He was a good man, if that makes sense. He had a wife and a family. He was everything I looked up to, not just on the pitch. I really wanted to be him!'

County lines recruiters have myriad ways of seeking out the vulnerable. Diego tells me that, unbeknownst to him, every foodbank he visited had county lines recruiters sitting in cars outside, marking out their next targets. It's horrible to think that they identified him as an option, then were probably watching him over a long period of time and therefore found out all about him. They knew exactly which school he attended because he was usually wearing his school blazer when he went. He thinks the recruiters saw him with the large picture of the footballer, which told them what his passion was. He remembers carrying it into the house with him, with such pride, and he remembers a black car that he also thought he'd seen outside the foodbank. The picture helped to give them the information they needed to get directly to him.

It started off with two Year 10 boys being friendly at school. 'They were in the year above and I didn't have many mates. Only one, really.' He smiles, ruefully. 'Jamie. But I didn't have time to worry about being popular in school. I was always looking after my brothers. I didn't mind looking after them, but I was pretty tired all the time.'

I ask about his mum.

'She was drunk.' He pauses. 'Yeah, honest. She was pissed every day. It wasn't her fault though. Not really. She started drinking because she was grieving and in despair, you know, because of Dad going and that. She felt that everything had gone against her.'

'I guess it can feel that way sometimes.'

'Maria, me auntie,' he continues, 'Well, not me auntie-auntie, but, you know, she tried so hard to help us. She got my mama to go to AA or something.'

I sigh. 'Oh, Diego I am so sorry. And did it work for her, the AA?'

'For a while.' He smiles sadly.

He explains how Maria and her friend, Beatrice, cleaned the house and got things straight.

'They were the dream team,' he sighs.

He tells me how Eliana struggled with simple stuff, especially anything online that needed passwords and account numbers. Maria and Beatrice set up most of the portals and pages for the school and helped her to apply for all the different benefits. But then they both had their own families to look after, and they both got jobs. Once they stopped coming round so often, it didn't take long before his mum slipped back into being sad all the time again. She got depressed once more, and this time it was even worse.

'Maria used to say that the Portuguese families all

feared depression like they used to fear the bogeyman when they were children,' he says.

Maria came back when she could, but it wasn't often. Beatrice wasn't around either. Diego and his brothers would see her when they walked past her shop. She waved and sometimes ran out with some cakes for the boys and Eliana. But it wasn't the same.

One afternoon, in early December, he came home from the foodbank to find Eliana sitting on the sofa with no lights on, even though the sky was already dark.

'It was pitch-black. I asked her why she was sitting in the darkness. She was in a really bad way. She flinched when I flicked the switch to turn on the light. She told me that she felt as if she wasn't just sitting in the darkness but living in the darkness. She said she felt as though she had nothing to live for. Christmas was around the corner and she had no money. Once, it was her favourite time of year but all the anxiety of Christmas and everything it once meant to her was too much to bear. The next day I came home from school and found a bottle of Lidl vodka wrapped inside a tea towel in a shopping bag on the back of the door, as if she was trying to hide it. It was worse, somehow, that she was trying to pretend that it wasn't happening again.'

He is so articulate and so candid as he tells his terrible tale.

'I wished that Maria – or Beatrice – would come back. But Maria was busy working extra hours for Christmas. And Mama was on her own. When we got properly into winter. Darker days, shorter. I tried to make her get up in the mornings, but most days she asked to be left alone. So everything fell to me again. But with my brothers to sort out, there was too much washing, too much cooking, too much mess. I couldn't keep on top of it.' He shakes his head.

My heart goes out to him. I know exactly how much washing, cooking and mess four kids in a household make.

'I'm not surprised,' I say. 'What a lot you had to go through, one way and another. This is so much for a boy – or anyone for that matter — to have to deal with. That's really hard. Nobody would manage it. You poor boy.'

He smiles. 'It was alright. I tried to do me best. But it was survival. It wasn't a life. And I wanted a life. Then these lads, they said they wanted to play footie. Now, I love football.'

'Oh, really?' I joke. 'I'd never have known!' But it's not the time for jokes.

'I mean, I *really* love football, it's where I belong. I feel free when I'm on a pitch.'

I can hear the passion in Diego's voice.

'And that's how they got me.'

'It sounds like these people prey on vulnerable people.

Like in the animal world where predators target young, sick, or weak individuals, the ones who've been separated from the herd,' I say.

'I was definitely separated from the herd,' Diego agrees, sadly. 'And I was young.'

'It works in nature, you know, natural selection. Lions isolate the easiest prey, and crocodiles do it.'

'Yeah, not to their own species though.'

'Very true. It's a good point.'

'And county lines isn't about natural selection.'

'No.' Perhaps my analogy isn't as good as I first thought.

'It's about dark crime rings and bosses who don't care about anyone else. Exploiting anyone and everyone they can – with fear – to use as slave labour. It's about greed. Profit. Maximum profit at any cost.'

He knows so much for a kid his age. I have to keep reminding myself just how young he is. And he is such a good kid, whatever has happened. Diego wasn't born to be a master criminal; it is something that young people like him are forced into.

'Go on. What happened with the boys?'

'At school I always had to dash off at the end of the day to get my brothers from school. But one day, I was heading through the corridor and two Year 10 boys walked through coming the other way. They sounded friendly enough. I actually wondered if they were even talking to me, or if they were talking to someone behind me, like, but the corridor was empty. The next day, the same thing happened again: Luke and his mate, Craig, were there. It was weird, because I couldn't remember them being around before that. But then I started seeing them all the time. I'd bump into one, or both of 'em, around school between lessons or at break and lunchtime. They'd always speak to me, which was also weird because, apart from Jamie, nobody else really spoke to me at school.'

'You were being groomed.'

He nods. He tells me how they asked him if he wanted to play footie after school.

'I was chuffed, like, but I couldn't do it after school. I mean, I couldn't even play for the team because I had to go and get my brothers.'

I think about all the sacrifices he has been forced to make.

'They said it was OK, we could play on Saturday morning, instead. I was made up. I got my boots ready and put them in a bag with my football socks. I was so happy to get away and out of the house for a few hours. Leave all that shit behind, you know?'

'I don't blame you. Leaving that world behind for a few hours, a kick around in the park, I expect it was just what you needed.'

'Well, now I wish I'd never gone. It was raining, I remember. I walked to the park in that rain. You know, that rain that feels light but actually drenches you?'

I nod. I know exactly what he means.

'I was soaking wet by the time I got there, but nothing was going to stop me from playing football and seeing who I thought were new friends. When I got to the park there were a few lads hanging around, but no one was actually playing any football. I felt like a right twat. Stupid for bringing my boots with me and taking it all so seriously. You know, I'd really built it up in my head. We did have a kickabout, but they weren't any good and they weren't interested. Then Luke asked me over to his house afterwards.'

Diego shakes his head again. 'I knew the house that Luke said was his. I'd walked past it loads of times. It was a bit grubby out the front, and a couple of cars parked outside, a black BMW and a red mini. Ordinary cars and it looked like any regular house. I'd already seen that black BMW outside the foodbank. But I just didn't put two and two together.'

'You can't blame yourself for that,' I say.

'There were other signs though. My mum always commented on how pretty the garden was. She would have loved to live in this house. But it didn't look lovely anymore. As we walked past the cars I saw all the weeds and litter. We went in. Luke had a key. The house was dark and grubby. The curtains were hanging off the rail in the window. The sofas were leather but looked dirty. I didn't really think much of it. Our house looked like a shithole when Mama was at her worst. And then I met Boris.'

He describes Boris: a dark-skinned man with short, dark curly hair and a beard, who walked out of the kitchen carrying a plate of food.

'He was short and he didn't look anything like Luke, although he was old enough to be Luke's dad. That should have been my next clue. Cos it definitely wasn't Luke's dad.'

He carries on with the story. They all sat on the sofa. Boris spoke in a strong accent that Diego didn't recognise. It wasn't Mediterranean. He thought it was probably Albanian.

'You the footballer, yeah?' Boris said.

This made Diego feel a little proud: that this bloke already knew of him and his football skills. Diego explains that he was someone who normally felt invisible, so to be 'seen' was a novelty.

'You a Liverpool fan?' Boris said.

Diego nodded.

Boris said, 'That's good, they're a bloody good team,' in his thick accent.

There were a few other people in the house: a woman

and another man who looked Arabic but sounded like Boris, with the same accent.

'But he was the one in charge. He was nice to me. He made out like he was looking after me. I sat on the sofa and he asked me about football. He even put football on the telly when I was there. It was great. We didn't have Sky at home. I only stayed for an hour or so that first time, then I went home. I didn't realise it then, but I was already lost. I was an idiot.'

My heart sinks at just how little it takes. A young boy who had already lost his dad and felt abandoned by him, and was losing his mum to alcoholism and grief. This Boris arsehole knew all that, and yet he sat there and made this boy feel that he had a father-figure in his life again. And he did it with hardly any effort. Complimenting his football skill. Turning on the TV. What a creep. What an arsehole. I wanted to punch his face.

Then I remember that these are Year 10 boys helping to bring him in. Vincent is in Year 10. I would be so horrified if I thought he was exploiting someone.

'What happened next?'

He tells me that the following week at school, Craig and Luke waved at him around school. Diego liked them. He didn't really have any other friends, besides Jamie, and they seemed alright. OK, so Luke's family seemed a bit strange, but Diego wasn't really in a position to pass opinion on that, as his own family was so dysfunctional. He was invited round after school again, but he couldn't go because of his brothers. Still, he wanted to go, he wanted to have a bit of life for himself. So he arranged for Andre to bring the boys home by himself – he'd done it before. It soon became the new arrangement, and it worked. It meant that Diego started dropping round the house each day after school. Boris would be smoking a spliff. Different people would come in from the garden shed. There was a back gate and an alleyway. Some came and went that way, some came through the front. There was always a lot of coming and going.

'Did you ever ask what was going on?'

Luke and Craig explained that different people lived there, and Diego took that at face value. Boris made a lot of time for him. They watched a lot of football together on Sky Sports and they all talked football. Diego got to know Boris well enough to ask him if he was from Albania. Boris laughed. 'No, no, I am from Bulgaria.'

One day when Diego came round, there was a box on the table in front of the TV. Inside was a pair of Nike Phantom football boots, the pro-ones, in Diego's size. Boris told Diego that they were for him so that he could become the next best Portuguese football player. All he had to do in return, was take a little train trip.

It seemed too good to be true.

After that, he was asked to carry drugs on the train to the countryside. There would be money in it. Money that he needed for his mum and his brothers, and it seemed easier than going to the foodbank. He became a mule. He learnt to jump the trains and travel for free. There was always a soldier or elder on the train, a few seats away, watching him. They made sure he did as he was told. They liked him because he was polite, and polite kids are easy to control. It didn't take long before he started missing school. Soon he was away from school more than he was there.

Christmas came and went, and by then he was already in debt bondage. Boris was no longer nice to him. In fact, Boris made him do things that he didn't want to do.

'What sort of things?'

Diego shakes his head. 'In private. You know.'

I think he must be referring to the sexual exploitation that was mentioned in the original referral. He's clearly not ready to say any more. I don't push it.

Diego tells me that he was sent down the garden to the shed. It was a large shed and inside, it stank. There were, on average, six or eight people in there, making and packing drugs. It was another thing he learnt to do. When he wasn't moving drugs, he was packing them.

I ask him about the day when he saw the murder.

'I'd been on the road with these divs. They drove me

to the trap house and left me there for two weeks. There was no getting away. My mum told me afterwards that she thought I was dead. The police were looking for me. I was one of those missing kids you see on Facebook and that. You know the ones I mean? Then, I s'pose, they must have stopped looking for me. I was bagging up smack, coke and crack. I was working all day and most of the night. Me and the other kids. We slept on the floor. Our hands and fingers were swollen, cracking and sore from all the chemicals, but they made us work anyway. The smack burnt my skin. It's evil stuff. My face hurt and my eyes were burnt, but they wouldn't let us stop working. I wanted to go home *so* badly.'

He pauses for a moment. Remembering. It was clearly painful at the time and the memories bring it back. I don't want to push this conversation. I can see that he's struggling.

'When you're there, they make you hurt other kids, to prove to them that you are tough enough.'

He swallows. His eyes are pink and his face-colour is fading. But he carries on. 'I was in the car with another kid. He was from the other gang. Boris's mate had took him, I don't know the ins and outs of that, but because he was pissed off about something. It's easy to piss people off in that world. Everyone had done a load of coke, including me. I was off me 'ed. Totally out of it.'

Now that we are here, we may as well try to step forward. When he pauses, I give him a little nudge. 'What happened?'

Diego looks down. 'I was in the back of the car. I'm not even sure whose car it was. Boris's boss opened the back door and pulled out this kid, who I didn't know, and was next to me. They were all wired, like fucking mental.'

He stops again. I nod.

'This other car came in front. I don't even know where we were. We could have been anywhere. We'd been driving for ages.' He has begun to cry. I put my hand on his arm.

'They took this kid out and held him by his coat in front of the car. All the lights were on. It was pitch black, so when I looked out the window I could only see what was in front. It was raining. The windscreen wipers were on. I remember the sound of the rain. Someone pointed a gun at this kid's head.'

The way he tells it, I can see it all. I ask him how old he thought this kid was.

'Younger than me. I dunno. Same age as my brother. Maybe, 11?'

I sigh and move my hand on his arm to encourage him to talk.

'They were shouting at each other. They had made this kid take coke. He was crying. They shouted, fucking this and fucking that.'

I sit down closer to him and wait.

'The gun went off. I put my head down and wet myself. I did. I was fucking terrified. They were shooting at each other. The kid, or someone, ran past the window where I was sat, and kept running. They were all shouting and going mental. It was dark and raining. Fucking chaos. So I opened the door and did what the kid did and ran off.'

The way he tells it doesn't quite tally with what Simon told me. But Diego's certainly very, very shaken in the retelling of it. Or perhaps that's not the full story. I don't think the boy did get away, otherwise this gang wouldn't be after Diego. Perhaps he can't bring himself to say exactly what he did see. And even if he closed his eyes at the crucial point, it still qualifies as witnessing a murder. Perhaps this version is the only one his mind is willing to hold – easier to bear, and easier to share.

'I just kept running. I don't know what happened to the kid. I didn't know anything until after.'

What an awful, senseless, incomprehensible thing to have been caught up in. No wonder he doesn't want to confront the reality.

'But I knew I was dead, too, if I stopped,' he continues. 'I ran for hours. I found an old car by someone's house and the door was open. I just stayed in there until the next night, tucked down behind the front seats with my coat over me. I didn't know what else to do. I didn't know where

I was. Eventually I got so hungry I had to do something. I walked by these old posh buildings and there was a police station. So I went in.'

I ask him if the police were okay and if he was well-treated.

'Yeah, they were. They were sound. They got me some food and clean clothes because, you know, I had pissed myself. I must have stank. They were alright.'

'So what happened next?'

'They spoke to Mama, and then the social got involved. I had a lawyer, and an advocate, or whatever they're called, and a responsible adult – who was a twat. They moved me to a foster placement for a few nights, but the people were shit-scared and just didn't want me there. Then Simon came to see me. He sorted everything out. Ross and Ben have been like brothers or uncles. They're sound. They get it. I honestly can't remember where I've been. Four houses, then here. Wales, I remember Wales because their accent is mad.'

'It's a hell of a lot to go through, Diego. I feel exhausted just hearing about it. That's quite some adventure you've been on.'

'Yeah, there's that too. Diego. I've almost forgotten I have a real name. It's mad. I am not Diego, but I have become Diego.'

I smile and put my hands on his arms. 'It's not forever.

You will go back to being you, when this has calmed down.'

Then he blurts it out. 'My name is Pedro!'

I look at him. 'Well, hello, Pedro. Pedro. That is a very cool name. It's nice to meet you.' Although it's hard to think of him as 'Pedro'; he is Diego to us.

Diego smiles. 'Thanks. My mama's dad is called Pedro. He runs a restaurant. My mum's a good cook. I miss her food.'

We sit together for another hour, as Pedro tells me more about his family, his home, his old life. He is very honest. He tells me that he used to worry that his dad leaving and his mum's sadness were his fault. His and his brothers' fault, just for existing. At other times he would blame England and wish that his parents had never decided to move to this country. He talks candidly about the racist abuse they suffered post-Brexit, about his mum's views on what a racist country it is now.

'I remember her watching TV when that guy Boris had a bus with slogans on it about how he would save the NHS, and going on about people wanting an oven-ready Brexit. She thought people were fools to believe any of it.'

He talks about happy times, about the picnics they shared as a family, about playing football with his dad, a holiday to visit grandparents in Portugal.

I am honoured to hear it all, but I know that I can't

share any of it, not even with Lloyd, just in case something slips out that shouldn't.

I hope to God that this nightmare ends for him.

But can it? Ever? Really? Perhaps he'll never be truly safe anymore. There will always be the danger that someone will find out who he really is. Through no fault of his own, Diego will always be on the run. And that can only work if he keeps a low profile. So becoming a footballer can never happen. It seems so unfair. More than that. Beyond cruel.

This beautiful young man is going to have to live with never having his dream fulfilled. Just because so many people want cocaine and other drugs. The carnage that these nasty criminals wreak is truly heartbreaking. This poor boy, this poor, vulnerable little boy. They have stolen his life, his magical future. Who knows? He could have pulled his whole family out of poverty. He could have been someone. Instead, he is trapped in this forced anonymity.

In his heart of hearts, however we might talk about 'one day', I think he knows it too.

When there are no more words, I say, 'Pedro, now you must return to being Diego. But I would love to talk to Pedro again, if he wants to?'

Diego nods.

'Now, are you hungry? I am. Let's see what's in the freezer.'

XIII

As to be expected, Diego's behaviour changes once he has spoken about what happened to him. Something has been unleashed.

On the one hand, he relaxes a little more. The poor boy was doing his best to hold it all together all of the time, but sometimes falling apart is necessary. On the other hand, the anger and hurt that he has been hiding starts to manifest itself in different ways, as it's allowed to come to the surface. He doesn't go out into the garden to play football and it has nothing to do with the weather. I think it is sinking in that football might well be off-limits forever. It's heartbreaking. He deserves to play football. But how can he, when he is and probably will be for some time yet, in protection? It just isn't possible.

Our conversation marks a turning point. And it isn't a good one.

Diego's behaviour begins to decline.

After making such a brilliant start at school, he begins to find himself in a few scrapes and battles. Unfortunately, the school doesn't handle it with any imagination or insight. I think they would be better equipped if they knew more about his background, but, of course, I can't tell them what I know. I leave that side of things to Simon and he is adamant they must know as little as possible. He has learnt from 'bitter experience' (his words), not to confide in schools, because they don't get it.

Schools are large places. They employ lots of people and people love to gossip. Simon repeats that he has only given limited information to Diego's school. It would only take one loose tongue and his identity could be revealed. It already doesn't help that he has a distinctive Liverpudlian accent in the West Country.

I know *why* we have the General Data Protection Regulation, GDPR. I understand that it's to protect the personal data of people and to make sure that it's handled properly and safely, and that individuals have a right to say how their data is used. And that's a good thing. But sometimes GDPR is a strange concept in reality. I have seen emails from social workers who forget to 'blind copy' all the foster carers' names. I have access to hundreds of email addresses that I shouldn't have because they have accidentally appeared in our emails. I can probably see all of the foster carers in the county.

When it happens, not just once, but several times, we get a second email asking us to delete it. But there's no check to follow that up, so who knows if that instruction is followed or not.

But if one foster carer makes a GDPR mistake, you can be sure that they will receive a hastily-organised visit from their supervising social worker and their manager, under the guise of 'support'. I find the words, 'we are coming to support you', mean the opposite. It is a veiled threat. They then stick you on a training session – which is why 'training' in my world has become a euphemism for punishment, rather than something to value. However, I digress.

I start to get emails from his teachers. They say things like:

Diego is not co-operating.

Diego has not taken time to think about the consequences of his actions.

It has been a challenging day for Diego and he has made some ill-considered judgements.

They're all passive aggressive phraseology for the same thing. Diego has begun to react when challenged. They come from the same areas of the curriculum. I have several of these notes from one of the deputy headteachers, whom I took a dislike to almost straight away. He has the obligatory beard and bald head that my own history teacher had back in the day. Another stereotype in the senior management of education. He looks like a coconut. I wonder what their annual conference looks like?

This particular deputy head, who seems to have been promoted very fast, has, by his own account, only ever been in education. He told us at the open evening, quite cheerfully and without a trace of irony, that he had been to school, college, university, married his wife who is a teacher, and only ever worked in education.

As far as I can see, that doesn't give him the right or the qualification to judge a 14-year-old boy who has already seen more in his tender years than that idiot has in a lifetime.

Diego is getting angry over petty rules, and who can blame him. There is no outlet for his anger. He can't play football, the one thing that he loves and makes him happy. He doesn't want to play basketball, or rugby, or cricket, or any of the other things that keep being offered. Football is his passion. It's not just about the game, or the particular skill he is gifted with. It's bigger than that. It's about his life. His dad, his memories, his heritage, his heroes.

I read yet another email about Diego's behaviour. I show it to Lloyd who rolls his eyes and says what I think.

'So, how does repeatedly sending him to Restart achieve anything? Diego and other kids get removed from class, sit in a separate room and do what, exactly?'

'Not much.'

'Restart' is the school's system for dealing with anyone

who is sent out of a lesson. It's called 'restart' because they're meant to get some sort of mentoring to help them transition back into their classroom. The trouble is, that doesn't happen. They just end up working in silence with other kids that the school doesn't know how to deal with. These methods are draconian.

And Diego is being baited.

There are a few 'popular white boys' who begin to target him. Perhaps it's jealousy. Perhaps it's because he's raised his head above the parapet in class. Who knows? But all that testosterone is boiling over. Diego lets go of the chess and Lego clubs and begins to be outside at lunchtimes and after school. The prowling alley cat that has been inside him is fighting to get out.

There is a fight after school.

I get a call to say that Diego has been suspended. He has broken another boy's arm. Vincent reports that the boy whose arm he has, allegedly, broken is 'an asshole, a racist, and a creep around girls'.

'Yep, I can confirm *that's* true,' Lily says, with a vehemence that leads me to believe she may have been on the receiving end of some unsolicited attention.

But it's no defence. 'Violence is never good,' I say. 'No one should use physical or verbal violence, whatever the circumstances.'

Vincent isn't finished. 'So what do you do, then, when

you're at school and the teachers don't do anything and a bunch of "popular" kids make your life hell?'

I can see that he has a point, if not a strong argument. *Aaargh*. Sometimes life is a conundrum.

I want to support the school, but I can't help but be on Diego's side. He's been through hell. A properly trained eye would see that he has probably developed ADHD or another form of neurodivergence which, for so many kids, is triggered by trauma. Even an untrained eye, a kind eye, would see that he needs help rather than punishment.

Recently, I ran a pilot for my charity, Spark Sisterhood. We had a group of girls learning life and employability skills. We got a couple of women in to work with them who were both neurodiverse, and who shared their findings with us. It blew my mind. Estimates suggest that 15% to 20% of the global population is neurodivergent.

It's a big, umbrella term that covers various neurological differences like autism, ADHD and dyslexia, and accurate data is hard to gather due to inconsistent definitions, stigma and diagnostic access. But, in mainstream education, that figure is much higher when you add the children who are born with foetal damage from drugs and alcohol, which, sadly, is up around the 8-10% mark these days. Then add neurodiversity triggered by trauma, which accounts for another 15 or 20%.

That's potentially 50% of children in school who

might legitimately be considered 'neurodiverse' at any one point. Half the school population.

And yet they are being taught a one-size-fits-all curriculum, delivered via a teaching methodology that only works for one in two pupils. So, which school should be regarded as the 'special school'? It stopped making sense to me a long time ago. The boys who are bullying Diego may have their own trauma at home or online. Perhaps they are influenced by all that Andrew Tate stuff. But the attempt to standardise the approach to behaviour and education is failing our children. Jackson was so glad to leave school when the time came. He had been bullied and resents some of what happened. Happily, he now feels free of those people and those days.

Since then, I have learnt that the kids responsible for bullying Jackson were all struggling in one way or another. But little attempt was made to get to the bottom of it at the time.

Another week, another fight.

After another email from Mr Coconut, as it gives me pleasure to rename the deputy head, I decide enough is enough. I pre-warn Simon, Ross and Ben that I am going in.

Simon says, 'God help him.'

I sit in the entrance area of the school, just after the morning bell has gone, waiting to be allowed through the locked glass doors. I'm on a soft, red chair in front of a table of sketchbooks. I love looking at them, but I also know that putting them here is paying lip-service to a cultural life in the school.

Art, music and drama are struggling to be given any weight on most school curriculums, at the expense of driving up standards in core subjects. As far as I'm concerned, that is wrong. We'll end up with only posh kids from private schools getting all the acting jobs. Imagine the privileged few having to undertake method-acting to allow them to play a working-class teenager?

I shudder to think about it.

We really need to give creative subjects priority in the curriculum, and if we can't, then we need to create another way for young people to soothe their souls and expand their skillset. There is hardly any let-up from phones and screens. This school is very proud that a tech company has given all the students a special tablet to work on.

No more paper, they declare, at every opportunity.

Great for the environment… perhaps? But not for the home environment. The result is that none of us can help our kids with their homework, because we can't easily see what it is they're actually meant to be doing.

Personally, I think schools should ban all devices, except for during the designated tech lesson. I embark on one of my favourite daydreams: writing my imaginary manifesto in my head, for when I'm Prime Minister and in charge of all things to do with children.

Just as I'm getting to the bit about nurturing creativity, critical thinking, lifelong learning across all disciplines, and recognising the long-term benefits of creativity for individuals and society, Mr Coconut appears.

'Mrs Allen,' he says, managing to make it sound as if I'm in some sort of trouble at the same time as he reaches out to shake my hand.

I take it, reluctantly, and then walk behind him as he leads me to his office, noticing a few late arrivals legging it to lessons.

I think of Diego, and what he told me about looking after his brothers. Mr Coconut calls out. 'Peters, get a move on, you're late again!' to some hapless boy.

I say, 'I wonder if you know *why* he is late again?'

Mr Coconut isn't expecting that and looks a little confused. 'I'm sorry,' he says, but in the tone of someone who is patently *not* sorry. 'Do you know him?'

'No, I don't. But I know a few reasons why children are consistently late and it's worth finding out if you want to help them.'

I think the tone has been appropriately set for this meeting.

We reach Mr Coconut's office, which is a poky little

room that might once have been a broom-cupboard. The days of plush offices in schools have long gone. He invites me to sit and then begins.

'Diego is a nice lad–'

I interrupt, knowing the 'but' is coming.

'Before you give me the shit sandwich, I need to tell you that Diego is way more than a "nice lad!"' I want to add 'Mr blah blah' to the end of my statement, but now that I've been calling him 'Mr Coconut' in my head, I have genuinely forgotten his name. Tricky.

He does ask, 'Sorry, what is a shit sandwich?'

I look at him with some amazement, since the 'shit sandwich' was taught to every educationalist I know. I explain that I worked in education. He looks pissed off at that, and then slightly incredulous, instantly managing to belittle my old career.

'Yes, a shit sandwich is when you put bad news in the middle of better news to make the shit more bearable.'

He says he has never heard of that before and asks me which school I used to teach at.

I look at him, so judgey, and know full well that I am being challenged.

I say, 'I taught in a university for over 20 years, but was also chair of governors for two schools during that time.'

He looks at me as if I've just insulted his mother.

'What do you know about Diego?' I ask.

My question is deliberately open-ended and he gives me an awkward elevator pitch answer. 'Err, well, he seems like a good lad, about average at most things, but unfortunately, his behaviour is on the decline.'

I sit back, lips pressed together and take a deep breath in through my nose.

'Diego is not his real name. He has come from police protection because he witnessed a murder while being exploited by a drug gang. Diego has three younger brothers who he took on caring responsibilities for when his mother had a breakdown. He only spoke to his mother a few weeks ago, for the first time in nearly five months. Diego is a gifted and exceptional footballer who, since living here, was visited by a football scout but, because of the murder, he is not allowed to play football publicly. Because he is so talented, he attracts attention and that could expose his whereabouts.'

Mr Coconut looks frozen for a moment. Then his hands begin to rapidly wipe the top of his thighs as he struggles to find a response.

'What could the, er, school do,' he clears his throat, 'to support Diego?'

'You can spend the extra pupil premium money that you get for his PEP as a looked-after child. Some will have accrued by now. You can spend it on a one-to-one football coach, so that Diego can play after school in private.'

'Um–'

'But he will also need another member of staff there at all times, because he cannot be subjected to any more possible exploitation,' I follow up.

'I see–'

'Oh, and I need you to keep this *absolutely confidential.* If any of this leaks, Diego could die.'

When I get home, Lloyd asks, 'How did it go? Did you get what you wanted?'

I walk past him towards the kettle.

'Yes, all good.'

XIV

After going through all of that and managing to get a one-to-one football coach organised, Diego is not turning up. Mr Coconut has been quite supportive, and so he should be. But I am worried for Diego. I can feel his anger rising and rising.

All the confidence, good humour and banter that arrived with him seem to have drained away. He isn't interested in hanging out with the boys and Lily seems to have stepped back.

This is when he needs people the most.

I feel so helpless. I understand every rage, every frustration, every tear. This is unfair, and I hate it when things are so unfair. I go round and round in circles, wondering how we can help find justice for Diego. I want to fight for him, but I don't know how.

It's impossible.

If we really fight for him then we are basically taking on criminals. And I can't do that. I don't have the tools, and they aren't the sort I want to be hanging out with. Nor can I do anything that would jeopardise the safety of the rest of the family. It is another conundrum.

Despite Diego's anger, he still looks out for the others.

Lily gets home from school first, Ellie in tow, and recounts the story. A boy in the year above has been pestering her at school. He has been trying to convince her that if he had sex with her it would be a good thing.

Diego overheard part of the conversation and heard some of the lines this boy was spinning – partly because, as Diego walked past, the boy didn't shut up because he didn't know there was any connection between Lily and Diego.

This is actually one of the things I really love about fostering: no one really knows who's who, which makes it a great way of keeping an eye on things. I'm afraid I do use them, ruthlessly, some might say, to spy on each other. I wonder what the social workers would say about that? But how else am I meant to garner important information?

In Lily's version of events, Diego got this boy by his lapels and told him, 'You keep your pervy hands off my sister. You wanna have sex with her so you can brag about it to your twat-head friends. Well, you can fuck off. She is way out of your league, mate.'

Diego's timely intervention briefly returns Lily to full swoon-mode, not to mention Ellie.

'He was awesome. I was right next to Lily when it all happened,' Ellie gushes.

The 'deputy for discipline' at the school, Mr Justice, yes, I know, you couldn't make it up, tried to punish Diego, but there was no way that Lily and Ellie were going to let that happen.

'We made a full report,' Lily explains.

Probably with a few embellishments, I should imagine, but the report apparently served its purpose.

'So the case is dropped,' she finishes.

'Thanks to us,' Ellie adds.

'Good work, girls.'

And it is, good work all round, as far as I'm concerned. The girls head back out again, pleased that order is restored.

When Diego gets home, he throws his bag onto the floor and stomps upstairs without a word.

But I have some news for him that I hope will help to take his mind off things. Well, I have news for everyone, but Diego first, and anyway, he's the only one in.

I haven't even told Lloyd. He's off doing errands for his mum: picking up more prescriptions, then arranging her B12 jab. I asked him once if he would run around after me one day as much as he does his mum, but it didn't go down too well and he shot me an evil look.

I knock on Diego's bedroom door. 'Hi sunshine boy, are you okay?'

It should have all calmed down about that idiotic

boy at school. I wonder where he gets the idea that it's okay to talk to girls like that. Oh, I know: Andrew Tate. And others on social media who are anti-everyone and everything, apart from themselves.

'Fine,' Diego says, sounding anything but.

'Can I come in? I have some exciting news.'

Diego looks at me with a raised eyebrow. In my mind's eye I see Manuel from *Fawlty Towers* saying 'Que?'

I can't keep it in. I have to tell someone. 'We're getting a puppy.'

His face breaks into a broad smile.

'Yes, I am so excited. Would you like to see a picture?'

I pull up the picture on my phone.

He looks at the puppy. 'Aww, she's cute.'

'You're the first to know!'

The boys come in together. I can hear them downstairs. I look at Diego. 'Come on, come downstairs and get a drink and something to eat to keep you going while I cook dinner. See how the others react when I tell them!'

He smiles again and I am so happy. I have looked after so many children who have been dragged away from their childhoods by unscrupulous, stupid and selfish adults. Every single time that we manage to slow down the adult-related crap and offer childlike stuff back into their lives, these kids grab it with both hands. We forget, I think, that children are having their childhoods stolen from them, left, right and centre. I looked after one girl who was off her head on cocaine and had been subjected to all sorts due to county lines, but when she was quiet and everyone had gone, she sat next to me on the sofa with her head in my lap holding her childhood teddy, snuggled up with her cat blanket over her.

Diego stands in the kitchen chatting to the boys, smiling at me, and desperate to let the cat – or rather the puppy – out of the bag. I can tell he is excited. Lily walks in too, which is good, because she and Ellie can sometimes be out for hours.

'Right, can everyone sit down for a moment?'

Diego behaves like he isn't already in on the secret and it's all new news. He is such a sweetheart.

''What's happened? Has someone died?' Jackson says.

I laugh and shake my head. 'No, the opposite.'

I hold up my phone and point the screen towards them. It's blank. The photo I wanted to show them has disappeared. I try it again. The picture is of a little black and white dog, the same pattern and colour as a Holstein Friesian cow. Big handbag ears and a beautiful face.

'Aww she's sweet,' Vincent says, but his tone is dismissive. 'Is it a meme?'

Jackson, cottoning on quicker, is wild-eyed. 'Are we getting her?'

Lily leans over. 'If we are, she's mine.'

'She? But I haven't said what gender the dog is.'

'It's a girl. Unless you're getting a dog from the LGBTQi community kennel. She's wearing a pink collar,' Vincent says, too smart for his own britches sometimes.

Jackson wants to know, how exactly, we are getting this dog, especially after I have said, several times since Dotty died, that we were definitely not having any more dogs. 'What happened to seeing Doug out? I thought that was the plan.'

'I know, but I've been thinking about it. Doug is depressed. He misses Dotty. He needs a new wife.'

They all think this attitude is awful.

'An arranged marriage?' Lily frowns.

'What if Doug is gay and now has some peace?' Jackson says.

I ignore him. I go on to explain how, this morning when I was taking Doug to the park we go to sometimes that requires a car journey to get there, I had just parked my car and was getting Doug out of the back when I saw my old hairdresser, Michelle. She was meeting her mum, who was driving a little blue Fiat 500.

'Michelle told me to move out the way, because her mum's not very good at reversing.'

'And this is relevant to the story, how?' Lily says. She is developing quite the sarcastic edge.

'Well, because I was fascinated by their collection of

King Charles spaniels. They were stunning. They had all come from a regional charity that rescues mostly dogs, but sometimes cats too. I told Michelle that Dotty had died and we realised that we had known each other for 13 years because she remembers me bringing Dotty and Douglas into the salon when they were puppies.'

'Get to the point!'

'I told her about Douglas and his mourning of Dotty, the howling in the garden, all of that. She sent me the link to the website where she got her rescues from, saying that she could thoroughly recommend them. But I couldn't look at it then and there because my phone was on the kitchen table, where I left it while I was walking Doug.'

'Could you possibly drag this story out any longer?'

'Thank you, Lily. When I'd finished walking Doug and encouraging him to play with other dogs, I put him in the car, drove home and immediately checked the link. Amongst the photos for adoption was our little friend here. When I read on, I found out that her mother was a rescue from a puppy breeding farm in Wales. Sadly, they didn't manage to save the mother. She died soon after whelping, exhausted and in a terrible condition, having been constantly pregnant and giving birth to litter after litter after litter of puppies. But they managed to save the puppies. This one was called Keira. So… I made an enquiry online. The phone rang within ten minutes. I was asked some questions. The lady emailed me with the foster carers' details. At lunchtime, another lady came around to do a house check and looked at the garden.'

'What garden?' says Lily. 'It's a football pitch.'

'Exactly. I think that went in our favour. She stood out in the less-than-beautiful garden that is now a sports field and said it was perfect. She also said that she had spoken to Michelle who confirmed that I could be trusted, which was nice.'

'I'm not sure how I feel about the name Keira,' Lily says.

'We can change that.'

'So when is she arriving?'

'We're going to pick her up on Saturday morning. Who's coming with me?'

Jackson, Lily and Diego put up their hands. Okay, that's a decent welcome committee, but I'm suddenly worried that Vincent is resistant.

'Vincent, are you okay with this?'

'Yes, Mum. I just can't come on Saturday morning. I have plans.'

Ah. 'Plans' must mean a girl in the offing.

'I hope she likes the puppy,' I say, with a little wink.

Vincent ignores the bait.

XV

Lloyd is fine with the idea of Kiera, although he, like Lily, is *not* fine with the name.

'Keira is not a dog's name. That's the name of one of Lily's classmates.'

As far as I know, it isn't, but I know what he means. It's too 'human'.

When I'm back in the studio, I shuffle through my CD collection. I need to re-pile them. I like to listen to a fresh lot every so often. When I say 'fresh', the reality is that they're all old, but I still need to hear them and I group them according to my mood. Today, I'm excited about the arrival of our new dog. My happiest time is always in my studio, making art and listening to music. I want something upbeat. I lift another five off the pile in the hall outside my studio and reveal a CD that I don't think I've listened to in about 20 years, *Wide Open Spaces* by the Dixie Chicks. That's it! 'Dixie' is her name.

Saturday morning arrives. It's an hour or so's drive to the foster family, a duration which obviously does not go unnoticed and somehow requires a stop off on the way. We get some coffees from the drive-through at the service station, although I'd argue it's debatable that what they order is even coffee: more like puddings in a cup. They gather up some 'snacks' to go with the coffee-not-coffee and suddenly I find that I've parted with £50.

At moments like these, I do enjoy quiet thoughts about how rich we will be when the children eventually leave home.

Diego joins in with all the coffee and snack-buying, very much part of the team, our little band of puppy-rescuers. He laughs and jokes and enjoys the banter with the others. The postcode takes us to a large estate, which looks like it was built in the 1960s. It's a bit of a maze, with looping roads laced with little cul-de-sacs. We eventually find the right place: it's a teeny-weeny house with a white door in a crescent of other teeny-weeny houses. There are more garden gnomes outside than there is space to put them. It's a little gnome city. They're everywhere. I've never seen anything quite like it. And neither have the others. It provokes lots of comments as we pull up.

'Wow!'

'What the–?'

'Is this for real?'

I say to them all, 'Come on, I'm not going on my gnome!'

Then Jackson gets me right back with, 'Is it this gnome here, the one with the white door?'

Diego joins in. 'Gnome worry, be happy.'

'Oh, very good,' I say.

I can see by the frowning concentration on Lily's face that she is trying very hard to think of one. She looks at a large gnome with ruddy painted cheeks, who has been positioned leaning over the fence and says, 'Hello, do I gnome you?'

We all cheer.

A very old, round man with a bushy beard that comes down to a point opens the door. I try to suppress a giggle.

I have no doubt that we are all thinking the same thing: Where is his fishing rod?

We are invited into a small, cluttered room, where the other human gnome is ironing. We stay standing, because there wouldn't be enough seats for us all to sit on in this teeny-weeny front room. Suddenly, Keira-Dixie bounces into the room from the garden, which I can see through the French doors is also tiny. She jumps up on the sofa behind me and, although I carry on talking to Mr and Mrs Gnome, I do it with my hands behind my back, playing with Dixie. She isn't interested in anyone else but me.

I have my dog.

Dixie is adorable.

She is a hound with her nose to the ground.

When we get her home, she checks out everywhere. She walks, well, almost runs around the garden, sniffing at speed. Apparently, the blend of beagle and spaniel is a cheap hunting hound. The hunting hounds I have seen tend to look pretty ropey. I can see that she has a disobedient side to her, despite being a complete squidgy fluff-ball. She will need a firm hand and, having this many people in a house, that won't be easy. It just takes one of them to want to be besties with Dixie to undo all the work by letting her get away with bad behaviour – and then I am back at the start again.

Now, why does this sound familiar, I wonder. Then realise I am describing parenting!

So I make it the rule that all training is done via me and they all have to follow. I know kids well enough to understand that they will snitch if another one of them breaks the training code, maybe chucks a biscuit, or lets her upstairs when there is a 'no dog' policy in place for the upstairs. I shall be keeping my eyes peeled.

Having said all that, Dixie could not have come at a better time for Diego. He, like me, falls for her instantly, and they are keen outdoor buddies. He is teaching her to dribble a ball.

'Ha!' I laugh when I see them playing together. 'You'd better watch out, she'll be signed faster than you!'

He laughs, too, but I try not to overthink about what

I have just said. The reality is, it's probably true. Should I have said it? I don't know. But it wasn't said with any malice, just amusement at the way they were playing. I sigh and look out of the kitchen window to see Diego lying on the grass with Dixie, yanking a now-flat football from his hand. He's laughing at their tug-of-war. I haven't seen him as happy as this. And all it takes is a bit of goofing around with a puppy. This reinforces my theory that children should be offered ways to extend their childhoods for much longer – and be able to dip in and out of being responsible and just being a kid. I should probably point out that when I say 'much longer', I'm not suggesting that they stay at home forever being mummied by me – oh no, I couldn't think of anything worse. But after all that Diego has been through, having some genuine, wholesome fun and enjoyment is a joy to see.

However, it comes at a (small) cost. As Diego runs around trying to train Dixie, Lloyd's phone keeps pinging from the security camera alerts. Even when Diego tries to keep her away from them, Dixie runs off in the wrong direction.

On the upside, since Dixie arrived just over a week ago, that evil ginger tom thug cat hasn't shown its face.

This Sunday, Diego has another full half-hour scheduled with his mum and brothers. I still sit off-camera, trying to stay out of the way. It's become my habit to do so. I don't want his mum to see me. Experience has taught me that a foster mum has no greater enemy than the foster child's mum. I have been on the receiving end of unfounded allegations, been lied about, abused and generally given a lot of truck from birth mothers over the years, so I choose not to engage. I don't want to be on her mind. I don't wish her to dwell on the fact that another woman is looking after her son. Even though, in this situation, there is no choice and no blame. Not to mention that it isn't actually the foster mum who takes a child into care in the first place.

But how would I feel if things were the other way round?

And I also understand foster care doesn't get great press coverage. In films and on TV, scripts tend to use the idea that someone will end up in foster care as a threat, like it's the worst thing that can happen to a child, when, in fact, it's often the best thing that can happen for that individual. But who lets truth get in the way of a good story? Why would these writers choose a new narrative arc, when they can keep pushing the same old one – and help change nothing at all?

Diego enjoys a morning with Dixie and some gaming time with the boys. He seems to have settled down again. I don't blame him for his recent angry behaviour. I would be angry if I were him.

After lunch, I get a check-in call from Ross. He tells

me that he spoke to Diego's mum yesterday to confirm that everything is okay for chatting later today. Ross, like Ben, is now a very familiar voice. Simon, too. They have just become part of the fabric of our lives. I make the mistake of asking Ross how many children they are currently responsible for protecting.

To my horror, he tells me that it's over 130 children across the country. Jesus. I was expecting maybe, like, eight, or 10. But 130, that's a tall order.

'Can Dixie be in the room when I talk to my mama and brothers?' Diego asks. He wants to show Dixie off to them, and her new trick. He has also been teaching her 'paw'.

I set up the room and bring in a drink for Diego. It's nearly 3.30pm when I receive the link from Ross and the code for the Zoom on WhatsApp. We assume positions. Dixie is not playing ball at all. She is busy pulling paper out of my wastepaper bin and shredding it on the floor. I need someone to remind me why I thought that getting a puppy was a good idea.

At 3.30pm we are into the Zoom call.

Nothing. No one is on camera. We wait, playing with Dixie for a few minutes. Still no sign. She can't have forgotten, surely? These meetings are too important for that. We wait some more. We get to 3.50pm and she still hasn't appeared. I message Ross. He asks if I can speak in another room. I go into Lloyd's office. He's on the stairs, working on the big sash window.

'Our worker couldn't get entrance to Diego's mum's house today,' Ross tells me. 'We've had to call the police to gain entry and find out what's happened. I'll call you back as soon as I know anything more.'

I don't like the sound of that. Nor do I want to be the bearer of bad news. I go back into my studio, to Diego.

'Your mum hasn't shown up, so the team from Freeedom are there now, seeing what's going on. You go and do something and I'll call you as soon as we know what's happening.'

He looks worried and doesn't say anything.

I find Lloyd and tell him what's happening. He tries to offer possible explanations for why she hasn't appeared, but we both know that this is not good.

I tiptoe to see the others and warn them that we are worried about Diego's mum and brothers.

Vincent quickly jumps on a game that includes Diego, as does Jackson. Lily is wearing a black facepack and has a hair-conditioning treatment on. She looks quite the sight, but she offers her kindness and asks if there is anything she can do.

At 6pm, Ross calls.

'We're in the house and the boys are fine. Diego's mother was out of the house earlier.'

'Oh, thank goodness. So, nothing to worry about. We just reschedule the call, then?'

'Not quite. Her mood is off and she seems scared. We asked the boys where their mum was this afternoon. They said they thought she was out with Maria because they heard a car drive off, but when Maria was contacted, she told us that she hadn't heard anything from Eliana for several days.'

'So, what does that mean?'

'Not sure. Although Eliana isn't sharing any information with us, we think it's likely that the gang are putting pressure on her to find out where Diego is. For now, Louise, just carry on as normal. We'll be over tomorrow to check the security and talk to Diego. We'll aim to be at yours at 4pm. Is that okay?'

I don't like this. At all.

In the morning, they all go off to school and college as they normally do. I spend the day catching up on the usual avalanche of emails that have arrived and walking Dixie and Doug around the fields. I was told off by one of my lovely neighbours, Pat, who, it turns out, trains dogs.

'Take the harness off and don't use the extendible lead. You have to train from the collar.' Right, well, that certainly told me. I am definitely seeking further training advice from Pat. And Dixie certainly needs it.

When I get back, I make a coffee and head to the

studio, but I soon head back to the kitchen to give both doggies another Bonio treat. I can't resist. I can hear Pat's voice in my head. 'Consistency, Louise, is how we train dogs.'

Does that apply to children, too, I wonder? Oh, if only life were that straightforward!

Our Monday night supper is bubble and squeak with the Sunday leftovers and a fried egg on top. Vincent used to think I was serving up the devil's vomit until he tried it with Daddy's HP sauce. Now he likes it. Diego loves it. And it's got egg in it, so even Jackson can be persuaded.

All have made it home by 3.15pm, apart from Jackson, who gets a bus to sixth form college; or at least he does if the bus shows up or manages to be on time. I've lost count of the number of times I have received stressed texts from Jackson asking for a lift. We are not even out in the sticks and the buses are, at best, inconsistent. It seems like a 'little' moan, but the reality is, I think, that poor bus services directly affect life opportunities. Someone dependent on a bus could miss an interview, miss important coursework, miss an exam, miss a medical appointment; anything, really. The only way for someone to ensure that they are in control is to be able to drive. Forget the environmental impact, have you seen how long the waiting list is for driving tests lately? People from London are taking driving lessons in other counties, because there aren't enough instructors.

Sometimes, I do think this country has gone totally mad. At other times, I think it's just the Allen household.

At 4pm, Ross and Ben are at the door. They don't look like their normal happy selves. Gone are the broad smiles and the chilled vibe we've been used to. I invite them in.

'Where's Diego?' Ben asks.

'Upstairs,' I explain. 'He's just gone to his room with the equivalent of a year's supply of crisps.'

There are no chuckles at my silly joke.

'Is Lloyd about?' Ross asks. 'We could do with talking to you both together.'

He's in his study. I go and fetch him. We all go into the kitchen. They turn down my offer of coffees.

Ross gets straight to it. 'We parked in the Sainsbury's car park about an hour ago. We needed to go to the toilet and Ben wanted to get some food.'

I nod.

'When we got out of the car, I heard a Liverpudlian accent. Obviously, we're on high alert for those. I looked up and watched as these big lads got into a car. I didn't like the look of it, so I took a sneaky picture of their number plate and sent it to Simon.'

Ben takes up the story for a moment. 'Simon sent the number plate to the police to check.'

My heart is already sinking. There's no way this narrative ends well.

'Unfortunately, it's a car owned by one of the gang that was involved in the murder Diego witnessed.'

Lloyd runs his fingers through his hair. 'What does this mean?'

Ben says, 'Basically, Lloyd, it means that they are in the area, probably trying to find Diego. I doubt they're here for the tractor trundle.'

Signs for the local tractor trundle are up all over the place. Ross and Ben will have seen them as they drove in.

I know the answer before the words are out of my mouth. 'We're all in danger, aren't we?'

XVI

The next few minutes are spent making plans.

'Because of the threat their presence clearly presents, we need to move Diego as soon as possible,' Ben explains.

'Today?'

'Yes, Louise,' Ross says. 'I'm afraid so. This evening. We'll stay here now, and we'll move Diego in the night. We have a few arrangements to make first.'

'Is everyone else home?' Ben asks. 'Could we ask that none of you leave the house?'

'I was just about to head to the shops to buy some ingredients for–' Lloyd starts to say.

I put my hand on his arm. 'Lloyd, don't worry. We can eat what's in the freezer.'

While Lloyd loves cooking, he is convinced that everything has to be fresh. I, on the other hand, grew up when a trip to Bejam (in the days before Iceland) was classed as a trip out, rows of chest freezers to be admired. 'We've got plenty in. Let's just do as they say.'

Lloyd nods, shaken.

Ross stands up. He looks at his phone and texts something. 'Is it okay to go and see Diego now?' he asks. 'We need to tell him what's going on.'

This is serious. My whole body knows it. My legs are trembling. 'Yes, of course. Let's call all the kids down. You're right. We need to tell them. I'll message Jackson to come straight home.'

Suddenly everything is different. Our world has shifted. It's like a war has been declared on us, or the bogeyman is coming.

This is real and this is horrible.

Ben asks Lloyd if he can check all the cameras on his computer. They go into Lloyd's studio. There is no laughter this time, no frivolities. I've been so annoyed by the pinging of those bloody cameras. Now I'm so, so grateful they are in position.

I call Lily and Vincent down; they reluctantly come.

I sit them down and say, 'Listen carefully. You can't leave the house tonight.'

They both look at me in unison and ask, 'What do you mean? Why not?'

'Because something has happened–'

'What, what is it?' Lily must be able to see the fear in my face.

'Ross and Ben overheard a few men talking in the car park at Sainsbury's. They spoke with Liverpudlian accents which, as you know, is unusual around here. Diego is the only person with a Liverpudlian accent in this area, as far as I know.'

'That doesn't necessarily mean anything,' Vincent says.

'In this case, it does. Simon did a number plate check and, as it turns out, the car belongs to someone in the gang that Diego knew back up North.'

Vincent's tone shifts to one of concern. 'Is Diego okay?'

'Yes. Ross is with him now, but it must be terrifying and I don't think they want to take any chances. So, I need you to hand your phones and tech in, please.'

This causes a far more disgruntled reaction than informing them that we might be under surveillance of a gang.

They ask why.

I avoid saying, *so we don't die tonight,* although I'm thinking it, and modify it to, 'Protection. Just in case any of you are being tracked. We don't know how they've managed to find Diego, and we need to be sure that we are all safe. So, no little conversations with Ellie – or anyone else. No one must know anything until Diego has been moved.'

Vincent says, sharply, 'Diego is leaving?'

'Yes, sweetheart. He has to. They need to move him to

another safe place. I don't know how the gang members found him here, but something isn't right. Somehow, they know he's around – and worse case, they might know where he lives – which is why we need to trust in Freeedom and their expertise. They know what they're doing.'

Lily bites her lip, pushes her phone across to me and goes upstairs to fetch me her iPad and her laptop. Vincent comes down with his consoles, his phone and laptop.

'Thank you. Well done for being so understanding.'

'What will we do?' Vincent asks, genuinely worried about how he is going to occupy his time in the absence of gaming.

I'm grateful for the invitation to laugh and break the tension, as I point towards the cupboard. 'In there are loads of board games. That's gaming, isn't it? Of a sort. There is also a thing called a *television* next door in the sitting room. Have you heard of that? We can all watch a film together.'

Now it's Lily's turn to laugh. 'What, you think there's a film that we will *all* want to watch?'

She does have a point, but we'll cross that bridge later.

'Yes, we can watch a film,' I say firmly. Not least because I'd like to have eyes on all my babies tonight.

Lloyd comes into the kitchen, followed by Ben. 'All good. We have every angle covered and there's no sign of anything untoward. It's all good!'

'Do you mind if I take a look around the house and check doors and windows?' Ben asks. He looks at the pile of tech on the table. 'Not bad!'

In walks Jackson. He takes one look at the tech, sees Ben and says, 'They know where he is, don't they?'

I ask the three of them exactly how much they know. We've never told them the full story about Diego, but they know way more than I thought they did. In fact, it turns out that they actually know more than I do. Jackson tells me all about what happened the night of the murder and why Diego is considered a witness.

I ask, 'Did he see anything, does he know who they are?'

Jackson nods slowly. 'Yep, he knows who they are. They know that when it goes to trial they'll be toast, which is why from their side it would make sense to take him out.'

I shiver at the language. The idea that Diego could be 'taken out'. But I had no idea we had such a budding Hercule Poirot in the house. Mind you, when the boys were little I did sit them down with me to watch countless episodes of *Poirot* and *Midsummer Murders.* They were, and still are, my 'comfort' programmes. I love them.

Jackson hands in his tech and claps his hands together. 'Right. Let's get busy and help Diego get through this.'

That's my boy.

Dinner is a buffet of pizzas, chicken Kievs and oven chips. Or 'freezer surprise' as it appears on my imaginary menu. None of us seems to have much of an appetite. Apart from Ross and Ben, who dig in without the need for a second invitation. After all, they can't leave or call for a takeaway either.

'The call could be intercepted,' Ben says.

And a gunman could turn up at the door, is how I mentally finish his sentence.

I take the dogs into the sitting room and give them some dental sticks to keep them occupied. Doug is delighted with his treat and settles in to enjoy it. Dixie's is gone in 30 seconds. I want them to act like guard dogs and keep a listening ear out as an early warning system.

Both dogs fall asleep.

Fat lot of good they are.

I'm not hungry in the slightest. I feel sick. I drink some water and encourage everyone to eat, even though I can't myself.

We all keep checking Diego.

'Guys, stop the side eyes, yeah?' he says, after a while. 'I'll be alright.'

After dinner, I load the dishwasher while they all decide what they want to watch. It's a painful process, and I'm pleased to avoid being part of the decision-making business. We end up watching *Friday Night Dinner.* Lily keeps likening me to Jackie Goodman, the mum character played by Tamsin Greig. I take it as a compliment, though I don't think that's how she intended it.

We all sit down on sofas and a couple of beanbags, borrowed and brought down from bedrooms. Oh, how I hate the beanbags. Those little white balls leak out endlessly from the big sagging bags, but I can never find out how. It doesn't matter how much I scrutinise them, I can never find the culprit hole.

Eventually, the kids go to bed. I am wired though, as is Lloyd. Diego asks if we can stay up with him.

'Of course we can.'

Then the others drift back in, restless, unable to sleep, unwilling to be on their own upstairs.

Ross has packed Diego's bags, ready for departure. They are by the door, but he had to put them there: we're all too scared to go near the glass front door in case we get shot at, or a load of hoodied-up men bash the door down with crowbars and slit all our throats with razorblades. My imagination is working overtime.

We all sit in upright positions on the sofas, gradually slumping into slumber until, at some point and some ungodly hour, I am gently woken by Ross and Ben.

'We're moving Diego now,' Ben says, his eyes alert, his voice a whisper.

I stand up and tap Lloyd's arm.

He lifts his head.

'It's time.'

We stand up, shaking sleep away. Diego is ready to go. Perhaps he didn't drift off like the rest of us. He has even more at stake.

I draw him in towards me. 'Come here, you darling boy. We are going to miss you!'

Lloyd shakes his hand, then hugs him, too.

The others, who are stirring and half-awake now, say goodbye and offer messages of good luck. Usually when we say goodbye to one of our foster children, we've had more time to prepare, and we're likely to see them again in the future. We can stay in touch. For obvious reasons, that will not happen in this case. Goodbye really must be goodbye.

There is a car waiting outside to take Diego to his next home and his new life, wherever that may be. Not in one go: they will change cars four times in the next few hours, in order to shake off anyone who might be following them. We turn the light off in the sitting room and peer out through the curtains, watching Diego get into the car. Ross goes with him, while Ben stays behind with us.

It all feels quite surreal.

'How do we know that driver is safe?' I ask, as if they haven't thought of that.

Ben says, 'Yeah, that's Mark. He's safe, he's alright,

he's one of us and he knows Diego. He's done this with him before.'

I send everyone up to bed, but I don't know how much sleep will happen. I still feel terrified.

Ben says that he will stay in the sitting room.

'I can sleep sitting up,' he promises, positioning himself with two phones in front of him on the coffee table.

At that moment, I hear a ping of the phone. I'm instantly alert. Who is outside our house?

It's our cat coming in, finally back home having run off for a while because of the ginger bully cat. I want to laugh, but just don't have it in me.

Goodbye, Diego.

XVII

Lloyd and I go to bed, eventually, after tea and toast and conversations that sound philosophical but are really just empty and tired. We know the truth. I managed to hide my tears from Diego, or at least very nearly; at the end, just as he was walking out of the front door, he turned around and saw Lloyd and me both crying. The poor bloody kid. What was his crime, exactly? How has his life come to this? Ben seems cool and unruffled. I guess he and Ross are used to the realities of this world.

Ben is not taking any chances. He is in professional mode and doesn't join in with our pointless musings. He actually tells us to go to bed, in the sweetest way.

'I'll stay up. Don't worry about me. I'll get my beauty sleep later. A relief worker from Freeedom is coming tomorrow to take over.'

We have three days of close security, then it will taper off as the message gets out that Diego has gone.

We don't know how his location with us leaked out, and probably never will. We all suspect school as the source. It wouldn't have taken much, just a few comments here and there. It will be his absence at school that will send the jungle drum back to Liverpool. They won't waste their time down here if they have no reason to, and we are too far away from the beach for them to have a little mini-break.

Lloyd smiles when I say that. 'Do gangsters have mini-breaks?'

I suspect their big bosses have yachts and speedboats. I imagine that a lot of their business is done offshore, quite literally. But what do I know? Quite a bit more than I did a few months ago, that's for sure.

For what's left of that night, I lie awake, listening to every sound. It's a horrible feeling, really dark. Not just fear, but the sickening knowledge that these predators are around, out and about in the world. It just makes me question everything.

I think about the school again and wonder exactly how the word got out. Whether it was a teacher – did I say too much to Mr Coconut? Or a kid, someone already involved in county lines. It's so clear that the schools are not aware about the reach of county lines. If they are, and I sent enough bloody emails warning them, then they are in total denial. I suppose it doesn't do to scaremonger, or make the presence of drugs in school public knowledge. Educational establishments are always worried about their reputation and even more so, I suspect, since the schools became academies. Perhaps they are worried about falling admission numbers. It seems to me that sometimes the reputation of the school goes before the needs of the children. They have become 'businesses' after all.

After an hour or two of tossing and turning I decide that sleep is impossible. On nights when I'm restless, I've found that the best thing I can do is get up and go downstairs. But then I remember that tonight it is not entirely my space: Ben is in the house.

I go down anyway. I can't sleep, or pretend to. I pace about like a cat on a hot tin roof. I peer into the sitting room to see how Ben is. He's in his chair with the cameras displayed on his laptop.

'Do you want a hot drink?' I ask. 'I'm making one for me.'

'Yeah, a tea would be great. Thanks.'

I go into the sitting room and sit on the chair. 'Any news?'

I'm relieved to see Ben smile. He's been so very serious for hours.

'So far, so good, Louise. No breaches here. Well, no human ones. I think your cats are becoming brave again, and so are a few other cats.'

I look at the camera images on his screen and see four more feline shapes in our back garden.

'They're all out there having a party now that the big thug has gone!'

We keep watching for a moment.

'I wonder where he *has* gone?' I say, meaning the cat.

'Like county lines, Louise, they do what they do until they can't do it anymore, for whatever reason. Then they move somewhere else and behave in exactly the same way.'

He's right. I hadn't thought about it like that before.

'So, if the policing was so good that we got them out of our county–'

'Yep, they move to another county and set up again.'

I think about this for a bit. 'But what if all the police worked together and adopted the same policies?'

Ben laughs. 'Now, Louise, you are talking sense. But who's listening? Trust me, with this many different police forces up and down the country, there isn't much room for sense. Or *joined-up thinking* as the saying goes.'

'It can't be that hard, surely?'

'If it was left up to people like you and Simon, we wouldn't have anywhere near the problem we have.'

I am really curious about this. 'So, each region does it differently?'

'Bang on the money. Yeah, because each county has a different local authority they have different levels of awareness about the problem, different levels of corruption. And not just a different budget, but entirely different budget priorities.'

'Hmm,' I say, still thinking. 'We know the gangs aren't stupid. They follow the news as much as I do. They'd know who the bankrupt councils are–'

'Exactly, Louise.'

'Then they know where to make their next move.' I shake my head. It does seem ridiculous.

Ben says, 'When they shut down counters in police stations and close rural stations, the gangs just rub their hands together. The politicians in charge are either badly advised–'

'Really, I can't believe that,' I say, my tone sarcastic.

'Or stupid–'

'Oh, I can believe that,' I say.

'Or, worse, they're corrupt. Whatever. For the paltry money they save from not having to pay a person to man the counters, they lose a zillion times over in court cases, legal fees, police time, the increased burden on children's and adult's social care. Let's not forget the prisons, and hospital A&E for stab and gun wounds.'

Ben hasn't been so forthcoming in his political viewpoint before. But things can be said in the small hours that wouldn't be said at other times of the day. He's off now.

'It was happy days for the gangs when the government

closed local stations. And now you have schools that don't want the naughty kids, so they're giving them away to gangs. Fuck me!'

He then apologises for swearing. He clearly doesn't know me well enough.

In the morning we all look dreadful from the lack of sleep. No one is allowed out, so the boys take full advantage of this predicament and order Dominos for lunch. Lily is twitchy. I think this is mostly due to her not having her phone though. All the tech is still inaccessible, locked in a big metal box.

I think I might buy one of those.

The sitting room has become an operations room for Ben who announces that two new people, Sandra and Steve, will be here in an hour's time to take over from him.

Ben also has other, grim news to share. 'Diego's mum was attacked last night, as were Diego's two younger brothers, Andre and Dinis. Part of the gang's campaign to find out where Diego is.'

'Oh my god, are they alright?' This is shocking.

'I'm told that they're all in hospital, and the social workers are splitting them up – putting all the boys into emergency foster care.'

I feel sick. It's all too much. Too horrible. I feel overwhelmed. Lloyd, who should – or at least could – be making me feel better, is on a panic-lockdown of his own, inside his study. I remind him that we are already on a 'lockdown', although this one has a very, very different feel from the way that word was used during the pandemic. Our lockdown is personal and it is unsettling us all.

I wish things were different.

To physically attack Diego's mum and brothers. It is so vicious and horrible. A woman and her children. It just beggars belief. But on the other hand, I shouldn't be surprised. This is county lines and they make their vast profits from the slave labour and exploitation of kids.

We are all out of sorts. I don't know what to do with myself. I try to play with Dixie in the garden, but my heart really isn't in it.

Soon enough, in come Sandra and Steve, Ben's cover. I introduce them to everyone and offer refreshments. They get straight to business. I ask why there are two of them.

'We normally work in twos,' Sandra explains. 'That's the protocol.'

'Last night was a one off,' Steve adds.

I don't know how people live under police protection for months, sometimes years, without going mad. We have only done one night and I already feel like my wings have been clipped. It's hard having this presence in the house, and being dictated about what we can and can't do.

Having said that, I take to Sandra instantly. She is like a teacher, but the best sort: commanding yet funny. She is very experienced. She was a soldier before she joined Freeedom, and tells me that she has done 12 tours of Afghanistan and been on active duty in other countries, too.

'Why Freeedom?' I ask.

'When I left, one option was doing a degree, but that wasn't for me.'

She tells me that she is a strategic thinker, so was offered leadership roles in project management and human resources. She considered the civil service, but dismissed it. Anything that put her behind a desk was out of the question for her. She knew she would miss the action.

'I thrive on field work. The idea of being in an office would kill me.'

Well, let's hope no one gets killed here, I think.

Steve is another kettle of fish altogether. He is an ex-con who has done time for GBH and robbery.

'Quite the pair!' I joke.

I ask Sandra how they get on.

'Steve's as good as gold,' she tells me, when he's in the sitting room on the cameras, and I get to chat to Sandra while I make her a coffee in the kitchen. 'He's a totally reformed man.' She pauses. 'He also knows I could kill him with one move, so he's a good lad.'

There's a twinkle in her eye as she says it, but it doesn't take away from the fact that I think she's only half-joking.

Each reference to 'killing', even as a joke, sits heavy. My mind is filled with images of these henchmen who are on the hunt for Diego. Who exactly are they? How old are they? What's their story? Are they all on the payroll of whoever it was that Diego saw? Or maybe the paymaster is above that person, higher in the hierarchy. This is all about money. Big, dirty, illegal, ill-gotten gain. I don't know why I'm picturing men all the time. They are almost cartoonesque in my imagination, but there is nothing funny about what they are up to. I try imagining that the top boss is a woman, but I find it harder to picture a female gangster. Maybe she's having a bad menopause. Maybe HRT would sort this hate out. It's all pretty dark stuff. In my more rational moments, I remind myself that hardened criminals really aren't going to be all that interested in us. We are absolutely boring and of no value or use to them. Nothing to see here. Especially as Diego is no longer with us.

'When do you think the kids can go back to school and college?' I ask.

'A few more days,' Sandra says.

I'm not happy about this, not at all, but it comes as no surprise that Jackson, Vincent and Lily all think that the enforced absence is brilliant. Something else I notice, and it happens almost instantly, is that all their moods have picked up enormously without their tech. Is it a step too far to attribute it to not having their phones? It surely can't be a coincidence. It's most marked in Lily, who seems to have undergone a complete personality change and is positively lovely. It makes me wonder if smartphones mess with girls' brains more than boys', for some reason.

Lloyd's less affected. He's at least able to carry on working. Most of his clients are overseas and on different time zones. I hear him say on one call that he is unable to leave home, and that there are security personnel operating in the house.

Who even talks like that?

I have entered a parallel universe, or I am slowly going mad. Either way, I actually hate this. I want to take my dogs out. I need the fresh air. I need some normality. Little Dixie needs a walk. It's quite difficult to explain the whole situation to a dog.

On day three we get the green light to leave the house once more, following a debrief from Sandra and Steve. We are advised not to take risks, and to make sure the security cameras remain on for the time being.

'But they are only a caution. We believe the threat to have subsided,' Steve says.

They have information that the car that Ross and Ben saw in Sainsbury's car park was later spotted on the M5 near Avonmouth.

'It could be heading to Wales, given the location. We're following it,' Sandra says. 'If they are heading to

Wales, though, they're wasting their time, because Diego is not in Wales.'

'Where is he?' I ask.

She glares at me.

I suppose I deserve it. It was a stupid thing to ask. I change the question. 'I mean, *how* is he?'

Sandra says, 'Okay.'

That is the end of the discussion. It is, perhaps, as much as we will ever know. He is safe. He has moved on. As a foster carer, children come in and out of our lives. Saying goodbye and moving on comes with the territory, but never has it come so brutally, so swiftly or so finally as with Diego.

The house feels strange when the team has gone.

I take down the posters and Liverpool gear from the room that was Diego's, or Pedro's, for the brief time he was with us. I look at the garden, changed forever by the boy with the football.

He certainly made his mark.

And, in his wake, we are left with the cameras. I become obsessed with watching the cats on camera until late into the night. Everyone else has gone to bed, but I can't drag myself away from looking at all the images on Lloyd's screen.

I'm sure I catch a flash of fur across the screen. That bloody ginger tom!

Epilogue

The Liverpudlian gang members who want to locate Diego have not gone away. They are still at large. And, even though Diego is long gone from our home, we are still scared. One afternoon, I hear a Liverpudlian accent in Sainsbury's and I'm instantly alert.

I hang back, listening, to find out more. It's okay. It turns out to be an old fella talking about his allotment. There are a lot of allotments around here; something I will never have. Most people I know who have got involved with one start with good intentions, then realise how much work and cost is involved and end up back at the supermarket.

When I get back home, I realise how intimidated I felt, just from hearing the regional accent. Perhaps I'll always have that reaction to it. That's how terrorising works: it's insidious – bullying, cranked up.

I miss Diego. I think we all do. He was, and I hope will remain, a good kid at heart. We found him to be a lovely young man.

I wanted, very badly, to say to his mum how proud

she should be of her eldest son. What a good person he is turning out to be.

I should have said it when I had the chance, because I didn't get another opportunity. Now we are out of the conversational loop.

Kendi has been great, back to his old, supportive and very kind self. We are so glad to have him back after he appeared to leave us briefly, in spirit at least, in the pursuit of management. I'm thankful that particular avenue of career development didn't work out for him.

But, through Kendi, we discovered that the tragedy of Diego's story has another twist to it. The friend of the family that Diego called 'auntie', Maria, had called in one evening and caught Diego on his way out of the house, back when he was already in the grip of county lines. She hardly recognised him. He looked ashen, gaunt and older. She was struck by his hands, how his fingers were swollen and sore – which would have been from packing drugs. As a result, Maria tracked down Duarte, his father, and told him what the situation was like for his wife and children. She didn't sugarcoat it, and also made sure his parents knew, as well as Eliana's.

She followed Diego to the house he was working in. She took a photo of the house and sat nearby in her car and watched the activity. She took more pictures and uploaded them to Crimestoppers. Then she went back to Eliana's and waited, but Diego did not come home. If only she had done what she did a little sooner, perhaps Diego's troubles would have been lessened. Who knows? What it does give me hope for is that perhaps Diego has an escape route back to Portugal. He has his father and grandparents there, and although the family have hardly had anything to do with Diego, perhaps, given the circumstances, they could be persuaded. At least he might be able to play football at a local level there safely. Diego once told me that while Duarte learnt a trade to fall back on and was able to find employment when his own football dreams fell apart, it meant that he was keen that his sons, especially his first born, who showed a talent for football, should follow theirs.

We tried to keep this episode in our lives as quiet as we could while Diego was staying with us. He wasn't with us for very long in the end and, apart from what I told the school, very few people knew much about him. Cinnamon, our lovely cleaner who comes once a week, was in on the secret, but is always very discreet, especially as far as our foster children are concerned. We did talk about county lines afterwards though. She has sons at local schools: one in primary and one in secondary. She told me about the way that county lines has infiltrated the secondary school.

'But this time, the leadership team has done something about it.'

Given how much I struggled to get a reaction from the school when I shared Diego's warnings and observations, I was thrilled. 'What is it that they're doing?' I ask.

'They've got a speaker in for the afternoon.'

Ah. It doesn't sound like much and I must look disappointed.

'No, no. It's had a big impact. He was talking very frankly about his heroin addiction and his recovery.'

'Right.'

'He had a rotten leg. Something to do with ulceration because of the drug. But it was wriggling with worms.'

'Wow. The worms should put them off, if nothing else.'

'Exactly.'

She also tells me that she thinks there are serious drug issues in our town. 'It has become a self-medication town. People are getting stoned just to get through the day.'

In our little town? Once I wouldn't have believed it, but now I do. I think about driving around that one evening with Diego, while he pointed out all the drug-related activity that was going on, hidden in plain-sight. Given that any illegal drugs distributed in the UK have more than likely passed through a county line, county lines are, literally, everywhere.

Afterword

Most of the stories that we tell in the *Thrown Away Children* series are the ones which have a good outcome for the children involved. If not exactly 'good' in some cases, then at least, 'improved'. Diego's story feels harder to tell, because that kind of outcome is close to impossible in this situation. Worse, Diego's situation was not even of his family's making. In fact, he did everything he could to mitigate it. His mother's loss and grief were not of her making. The collapse of her support network during the Covid pandemic was inevitable, perhaps, but what happened to them all was out of their hands. And yet, the full consequences for the whole family were devastating. I think that's part of what makes Diego's story particularly tragic.

We seem, as a society, to be very quick to blame others for things that they are not responsible for, as Diego's family discovered to their cost, after the Brexit referendum. There is a cruel irony in the fact that Duarte brought his family to the UK in search of a better life, but his plans were thwarted.

People who fear difference turned to blame during the pandemic, when there were shortages of goods in supermarkets. That led, indirectly, to Duarte leaving the country. He was not alone. Britain experienced a huge drain in the workforce in the post-Brexit period. Some UK citizens were encouraged to believe that the reason they were unemployed or in low paid work was due to the number of 'foreigners' employed here, but the reality is that after Brexit, when so many workers left, industries were left depleted. Eliana blamed herself at times for her husband leaving, but she isn't the one who created Brexit, or the climate in which Brexit could take place, or the shift in attitudes it seems to have marked.

Eliana tried all that she could to keep it together, but the supermarket hours she worked were impossible to manage alone with a young baby and no childcare. Diego stepped up to help with school drop-offs and pick-ups. He worked so hard to keep his family and 'be the man' in the absence of his father. We found him, always, the cheeky chappie, but the more I learn about him, the more I realise, aside from his footballing prowess, what a remarkable young man he was. He was also so mature and personable. He had evidently been raised to be polite, well-mannered and helpful.

I think another thing that made it harder for Diego in the first place was how much he tried to bottle things up – and that's a direct product of a society and culture that still operates within patriarchal notions. The idea that he, as the first born, had sole responsibility to step up and be 'the man' in the family is toxic for male mental health.

Taking on the caring responsibility for his brothers meant that Diego isolated himself from his friends – a dangerous position to be in. Feeling unable to ask for help because he believed he needed to be strong is a mindset that we have to change.

Acknowledgements

None of this would happen, of course, without Lloyd, Jackson, Vincent and Lily. I'm grateful first and foremost to them, my family, who are willing to take on the challenges of foster caring and, in this case, its very real dangers.

Thank you to one of the most important members of my team, Theresa Gooda, who uses skills I do not possess to bring these stories alive. She is always there on the other end of the phone to chat through the twists and turns of each story.

Then there are more people, the readers who all look for different experiences, emotional, structural and factual: Catherine Lloyd, Alexandra Plowman and Karen Furse. They see the first messy manuscript and have been with us for the whole Thrown Away Children series; their skills and insight are invaluable.

To Jane Graham Maw, my very special agent, who has always got my back; to my editor, Jo Sollis, who makes suggestions with such kindness; to Christine Costello for the book production and to Claire Brown for marketing and PR: thank you all. Thank you to Mirror Books for your continued support. You are all my brilliant team.

THROWN AWAY CHILDREN
OTHER BOOKS IN THIS SERIES

MILO'S STORY

Louise Allen

with Theresa McEvoy

Michelle and Andy are thrilled to be fast-tracked into fostering and are quickly paired with 7-year-old Milo

But Milo tears through their home like a raging tornado, destroying a beautiful interior – and their lives.

What are the secrets of his violent and destructive behaviours? Experienced foster carer Louise Allen steps in. Can she uncover the little boy's disturbing past and help him?

THROWN AWAY CHILDREN
OTHER BOOKS IN THIS SERIES

SPARKLE'S STORY

Louise Allen

with Theresa McEvoy

Louise gets a frantic call to take in a damaged and destructive young girl. Separated from her siblings Sparkle is hostile and angry.

A short while after settling in Sparkle begins to identify as pansexual. A revolution is underway in the Allen household, with Sparkle's transition motivating all of the young people to explore what becoming an adult means for them and the language and communication between everyone is in uproar.

But it's Sparkle's escalating behaviour that causes concern.

SLAVE GIRLS

A BRAND NEW LOUISE ALLEN SERIES

SLAVE GIRLS

Louise Allen

with Theresa McEvoy

Charlotte - The Cutting Girl - comes from a family of high achievers. Her father is a politician, and her mother is a senior medical officer.

When she moves from her prestigious boarding school she is groomed by a girl two years her senior, spiralling into a cycle of drugs, self-harm and sexual abuse.

When she goes missing, five other girls do, too. A nationwide media campaign sets out to track them down, but can Charlotte ever escape the gang behind the abduction and abuse?

THROWN AWAY CHILDREN: OTHER BOOKS IN THIS SERIES